More Dusty Trails

Glorianne Weigand

Happy Trails

Glorianne Weigand

ISBN 0-9644141-1-2

Published by
101 Ranch
Star Rt. 2 Box 31
Adin, CA 96006

Printed by • Maverick Publications, Inc.
P.O. Box 5007 • Bend, Oregon 97708

Table of Contents

Dedication

I dedicate this book to our four little Weigand buckaroos. Tyler, Shauna, Adam and Blake, our Grandkids that we are pretty proud of.

Also to the people that gave their time for me to interview them to write another edition of *Dusty Trails*. Sharing their stories of their families and themselves for everyone to enjoy.

Cover Photo
Leventon Blacksmith Shop, Lookout, California, built in 1888 and still standing today. Boy on left is Donald Leventon, Joe Leventon is the second man from left and Bill Whithall is on the horse. Others unknown.

Grandma Wiley, Sam's mother.

Sam, Norris, Mildred, Orrie and Harold, the Gerig cousins.

The Home of Generations

He's a regular little Sammy. That is what Will Gerig said about his son Oral when he was very small. Sam Smith was a friend of Will's and little Oral acted just like him so the nickname stuck. To this day Oral Gerig is known as Sam and most people think this is his name.

Oral was the youngest son of William Henry Gerig and Grace Criss Gerig. He was born in 1915 in the house he still lives in with his wife Gertie. Like his father raising his children in this house, this is where Sam and Gertie raised their children, Robert and Vicky Sue. Sam's mother left the family when he was only four years old so he was raised by his older sister Mildred Gerig Walker and his father. The other children in the family were sister Wilhelmenia, (Willie) and Orras, (Orrie). Orrie lost his life in a hunting accident in 1946 when he was 34 years old. Orrie left his wife Mary and their small son Dale. Willie married James W. James while he was in the service.

The home on the Gerig ranch was built in 1903. Mildred married Frank Harbert and stayed on the ranch to run the ranch home for her father and care for her smaller sister and brothers, and raised her own son Donald. She later married Floyd Walker and they built a motel in Bieber.

Grandpa William Gerig, Sam's grandfather was born in Wassen, Switzerland in 1847. His elementary education ended at the age of twelve and he became self supporting. In his teenage years he migrated to the United States and settled in Missouri. In 1871 when he was twenty-four years old he came by the way of the Isthmus of Panama and settled in Lassen County California.

In 1870 another family came to California, traveling by wagon train across the vast plains. The family, the Carmichaels, also settled in Lassen County in Big Valley. Mr. Carmichael started the first sawmill in Big Valley. He operated this sawmill for a quarter of a century. Mr. Carmichael had a daughter named Sarah and she became the bride of William Gerig in 1872. The Gerig's settled in Bieber where their first three children were born. Will was born in 1873, he is believed to have been the first white boy born in Bieber. Lena was born in 1875 and Nancy was born in 1878.

William Gerig then homestead a 160 acre homestead north of Bieber and built a home where the rest of their eleven children were born. Millie was born 1880, Charles, 1881, Henry, 1883, Etha 1884, Emma, 1886, Birdie, 1891, Peter, 1893, Ketura, 1895. William then purchased another 600 acres and added this to his growing ranch.

A dairyman by profession Mr. Gerig had many milk cows. He raised the hay for his cattle and milked many cows taking his milk and cream to the cheese factory in Bieber. A large family to raise was a big job. But one that William and Sarah did proudly and well.

William Gerig was a self made man and was well respected in the valley. William built his ranch without any resources other than his own industry. Mr. Gerig passed away February 11, 1898, leaving his wife with a large family and ranch to run. Sarah was a strong woman and did exceptionally well. Her oldest son Will Gerig was 25 years old at the time and helped his mother run the ranch.

Around 1902 when Will was ready to get married Sarah gave him 160 acres to give him a start. He moved to the north part of the ranch that she had given to him and in 1903 started to build the home that his son Oral (Sam) still lives in today.

The Gerig children, Mildred, Willie, Orrie and Oral had to go to Bieber to school. Their father would saddle the horses and wait at the gate for the children to jump on and be off to town. It was a three mile ride and sometimes pretty cold. They would tie their horses in the livery stable in town or put them in a barn near the school and go to their classes. At the end of the day in stormy cold weather they would just wrap the bridle reins around the horn, duck their head and hold on as the horses would head home, "lickity split." Will would again be waiting at the gate and catch the horses and take them to the barn while the half frozen Gerig children would head to the house.

The school at Bieber had all eight grades and around forty students. Some of the kids that the Gerigs went to school with were, their cousins, Dorotha Gerig Kramer, Norris Gerig and the Hayes boys.

Others at the school were Kenny Holl, Ernie Wardwell, Ralph Gearhart, Gerald Packwood, Virginia Packwood, Birdie, Art and Jim Piercen, Margie Oaks, Mick Jones and the Stevenson kids.

Some of the teachers were Mrs. Loomis, Arad Way and Edison Lakey. A lot of hookey was played and the favorite place to spend their time was at the cheese factory where Don Moss was the owner.

Will Gerig and
grandson Robert.

Sam Gerig.

Will Gerig ran a few dairy cows then started raising roan durham. He started taking his cattle to the forest to graze in early times before the forest service was even started in 1916. The cattle now range on what is known as the Crank Springs allotment and some of the area that was devastated in the huge forest fire several years ago. The Criss place that was the homestead of Grace Gerig is in Gougersneck and it now belongs to Norris Gerig.

Will Gerig ran around one hundred and twenty-five cows, and Sam now runs around 200 with the help of his son Robert.

Sam started early in the ranching business. His first job was to drive derrick team for Charles Canyon. He drove a single horse through the barn to pull the hay nets up. Sam was so little he couldn't manage the horse and she drug him around. He said he guessed you could say he failed his first job.

The next time he drove derrick was for his dad. He had one horse and a single tree. He would pull the net up and turn the net loose then hold on to the mare's tail and ride the single tree back to the field. Sam said the old mare knew more about it than he did. Will was putting up a couple hundred acres of hay. Now Sam owns 500 acres on the home side of the road and he and Robert put up the hay and hire some men to build the stacks for them. The Gerigs have a forest service permit and the rest of their permit is on private ground.

When Sam was a little tike he would love to go over to his neighbor's, Merlin Kennedy and help him herd his one hundred head of sheep. Merlin would give little Sam a chew of his tobacco and teach him to roll cigarettes.

A lot of Will's cattle would stray to the Huffman ranch near Tulelake. So when Sam was quite young this was where they would have to ride to so they could bring their cattle home.

When Sam was sixteen years old he went on a five day, seventy mile cattle drive with the Hunt ranch to take their cattle from Big Valley to Oak Run for the winter. November 1931 Sam helped them drive one thousand head of cattle the long cold drive. The first day they would drive them to the ranch store near Nubieber. The second day they would drive them over Big Valley Mountain and spend the night at the Albaugh ranch near Pittville, the next day they would go on to the Knoch ranch, then the Rising River ranch on Hat Creek. The next stop would be the Doyel ranch, then the Hanes ranch, then the Bidwell ranch at Montgomery Creek. At all the stops they would either feed the cattle hay that they bought from the rancher or graze them. The rancher would put the cowboys up for the night and feed them. Some of the drives may only be three or four hours, but the next stop would be too far for a one day drive. When they would get to the Oak Run road Bob Bartell would tell the cowboys to just let them go. The cattle knew where they were going now.

It was pretty miserable and cold going over Hatchet Mountain. They were on the top of Hatchet Mountain at the time the golden spike was driven at the railroad in Nubieber connecting the Great Northern and the Western Pacific. A historical moment for the small town in northern California.

Bad weather could always hit at a moments notice in the northern country of Big Valley. One time Sam and his cousin Norris Gerig decided they wanted to go to Nubieber to the show. The weather wasn't that bad, they didn't think, but they were the only ones at the theater. On the way home they got stuck in a snow drift and Sam had to spend several days with Norris. Will Gerig and Alvin Herrick were left to feed the cattle and the snow was so deep all they could do is throw the hay out of the barn window and the cows just took what they could get.

Sam met another student at the Bieber school when she came here from Bandon, Oregon as a freshman. Gertrude Jackson took Sam's eye and they started courting. In 1938 when they went to Fresno to visit Sam's sister Willie they decided to get married while they were there.

Sam and Gertie moved to the ranch house that he was born in and lived there with Sam's father Will. Will was still very active on the ranch and it was a busy household. Will passed away in 1965 at 92 years of age. Sam has never lived in any other house in his life.

As all ranchers the Gerigs used to feed with a team of horses, but Sam bought his first John Deere tractor during World War I. As there was a rubber shortage, the tractor had synthetic rubber tires on it. Mr. Bethel at Fall River Mills where the Gerigs bought the tractor would not guarantee the tires. The John Deere cost them $900.00. Today the tractor sits in the shade with the original tires on it that they could not guarantee.

Sam was called into the draft, but never had to serve in the service because he was a rancher and had to stay home to provide the beef for the army.

A love of Sam's life has always been hunting. Deer hunting has been his favorite. Traveling to Nevada, Idaho, Montana, and Oregon he has many fond memories of the past years of hunting with his brother Orrie, Gerald Packwood, Dolin Southard and Kenny Holl. Sam has killed a buck every year, but this year he didn't even get his deer tags.

Robert and his wife Janelle live on the ranch in their home and Robert help's his parents run the ranch. They have four daughters.

Vicky Sue lives in Medford, Oregon and enjoys her work there.

The Gerig family are known for their longevity. Peter Gerig, Sam's uncle lives on the original Gerig homestead, in the house where he was

Sam and Robert Gerig.

born in 1893 and is now 101 years old. Sam's aunt Birdie was born in 1891 and is 103 years old. The rest of their brothers and sisters lived into their ninetieth years.

Running the ranch and raising cattle is really all Sam ever wanted to do, and he has done it well. The Gerig ranch is a picture perfect place to visit and Sam and Gertie make you feel most welcome.

Sam has worked hard in the community and has quite a few credits to his name. He was a bank director for the Shasta County Bank for twenty years, a director for the Future Farmers of America for ten years and nominated honorary chapter farmer, a fire commissioner for fifteen years and belongs to the Cattlemens Association.

Gertie has been secretary of the Bieber Chamber of Commerce for thirty years and volunteers at Mayers Memorial Hospital two times a week. Always active in church, PTA and community affairs and the school. Gertie believes you have to earn a right to have a say in the community or school.

The Swiss dairy farmer William Gerig left his mark in Big Valley. His grandchildren, Dorotha Kramer, Norris Gerig, Mildred Walker, Herb Hayes and Oral Gerig are still in Big Valley to carry on the sterling worth and upstanding quality that William and Sarah Gerig were known for.

Glorianne Weigand
September 15, 1994

Oral (Sam) and Gertie Gerig on their 50th anniversary.

W.H. Lee Ranch Home.

A Fast Black Horse and Pearl Handled Pistols

"Go west young man", this is what Doctor Elbert Lee of Kentucky told his young nephew William H. Lee in 1887. William, (Bill) was not well and this seemed to be the cure for a lot of ailments. Doctors in the east and the south thought the drier climate of the west was the thing to cure a lot of people. Bill was born to Andrew Jackson Lee and Francis Lee in Kentucky September 5, 1862. Andrew's brother, Henry Lee, known as "Light Horse Harry" in the Revolutionary War was the father of General Robert E. Lee. This made William H. Lee and the famous General Lee cousins.

In 1887, twenty-five year old William left his father and five brothers and one sister and headed west. His mother had passed away the year before. One brother Richard Franklin came to California later, but the rest of the family lived and died in Missouri.

William H. Lee boarded the train in Kentucky and came west to San Francisco. He then caught a ride with someone that had a team and wagon and traveled to the town of Sisson, California. The name of Sisson was later changed to Mt. Shasta. There, Bill Lee bought a black horse and traveled on to Bartle and then on to Bieber in Lassen County. Lily Schott and her husband Fred were some of the first people he met. Mrs. Schott told Bill's granddaughter Annabelle Kelly in later years that Bill came riding into Big Valley on a mighty fast black horse with two pearl handled pistols strapped to his hips.

Bill found a job on the Cox and Clarke ranch near Bieber, and worked there for several years. In 1889 Bill married Lillian St. John of Bieber. Lily and Fred Schott stood up with them and they were married in a home in Bieber. They then moved east of Bieber to a place owned by Andrew Babcock.

Lillian was born at Millville, California June 22, 1872. She and a twin sister Nellie, attended school at Millville. In 1880 when she was

W.H. Lee Ranch Home with William, Blanch, Lillian, John, Alice, Bill, Nora, Wanda, Mary, and Elmina.

18

W.H. Lee and Lillian St. John wedding picture, 1889.

eight years old she moved with her family to "Chalk Ford", which was later named Bieber in Lassen County.

After Bill and Lillian were married they rented a ranch and started dairying near Bieber. Four of their children were born at Bieber. Elbert born in 1891, Wanda born 1894, Blanch born 1896, Elmina born 1897.

Bill and Lillian decided they wanted to have a place of their own so they decided to move over the hill to Fall River Valley. They left many good friends at Bieber where they faithfully attended the Community Church of God. They still stayed friends with the Studleys, Thompsons, and Schotts of Big Valley for many years to come. The Lees still returned to Bieber to church whenever they could.

In 1899 the Lee's moved to the Cole ranch on the bench that is now the Cruikshank ranch. After living there for a year they bought 320 acres of land closer to McArthur. This was known as the Davidson and McDermit ranch and the purchase price for the 320 acres was $3,500.00. A Mr. Peterson from Pitville became a close friend of Bill Lee's and he loaned the money to Bill to buy the ranch. Mr. Peterson had a big mustache and beard and always drove his horse and buggy around the valley. He would come by in time to give the Lee children a ride home from school and would always give them some coins that he had in his pocket.

After much litigation, the Lees cleared a clouded title to their property, a greater portion of it was a tule swamp. After much hard work and many sacrifices, they converted this into a productive ranch.

After moving to the Fall River Valley the rest of their family was born. All with only a mid-wife in attendance. Alice was born in 1899 in Pittville. John was born in 1901, Mary in 1903, William Henry II in 1906, Lenora in 1908 and Frank in 1911. The last five all being born on the Lee ranch. A family of ten children and the two parents made an even dozen around the dinner table.

In 1910 a large home was built to accommodate the large Lee family. The two story home still stands today and has been restored as near to the original state as possible.

A barn was built behind the house and as it was nearing completion one of the carpenters was working on the roof. "An enemy", as Mary tells, "came riding in on a fast galloping horse and shot the man off the barn murdering him in front of the other workers. The man with the gun spurring his speeding horse escaped and they never knew who he was or why he shot the builder." The barn later burned, and they never knew the reason why.

The Lee children went to school at the Pine Grove School which was a mile and a half from their home. They walked in the good weather and the older boys drove a team and wagon in the bad weather when there was a lot of snow. Some of the children at the school were the Tottens, Cessna, Starts and Arnolds along with the Lee children.

Some of the teachers were Edna Guthrie and Mrs. Lydia Joiner. Blanch Lee taught her sister Mary when Mary was in the seventh grade in 1916.

Some new boys came to school that the Pine Grove students did not care for. The boys at the school tied the new boys horse in the woods and put their wagon on the roof of the school house. With ropes and a lot of hard work the boys got the buggy onto the porch then onto the top of the school house. This still brings a hearty laugh to Mary as she tells of this trick they played. Hopscotch and ball were the favorite games the students played when they weren't playing tricks on someone. There were nine grades at the school with only one room and one teacher.

Mrs. Joiner lived close to the Lee's and drove her horse and buggy to school. If the Lee children would cut across the field sometimes they could catch a ride with their teacher.

Mary always enjoyed school and especially the Christmas parties they used to have. They had a tree and made paper chains and strings of popcorn to decorate it. All the families would come and they would have a huge pot luck dinner and Santa Clause would visit, and they would sing Christmas carols.

Christmas at home was quieter and Bill Lee would read out of the Bible then they would open their presents. Later the family added a pump

Lee Ranch harvesting, McArthur, California, 1915.

organ to the family living room and Blanch learned to play it. This was a treat to the family. Later all the girls learned to play the piano and were threatened with a buggy whip if they did not practice.

In 1924 the Lee's bought additional surrounding land, the ranch then comprising of 1,280 acres. The land was irrigated from large springs of unbelievable size that originated near the family residence, and furnished gravity flow water for the greater portion of the ranch. A Fall River irrigation district was formed but Mr. Lee had all the water he needed so he was not interested in joining.

Bill and Lillian Lee increased their ranch and cattle operation to over three thousand acres and supported a thousand head of good hereford cattle, and many good horses. Bill had bought 1,320 acres of spring range on the bench on the south slopes of Big Valley Mountain. Here the grass started very early and the cattle were driven there in the early spring as soon as there was enough forage for them to eat. Later he sold a right of way to the state to put a highway through and it split the property.

Cattle summered on private land leased from the Red River Lumber Company, public domain and forest service.

In later years Bill Jr. and John bought summer pasture at Widow Valley.

With an operation of this size and that many cattle it took a lot of hay to feed them through the winter. It took a lot of men and many teams of horses to put the hay up in the summer. Twenty to twenty-seven men were hired during the haying season. The Lee children also worked. The girls drove derrick and helped do the cooking and the boys worked in the hay field. A large dining room table was set for the hay crew and the Lee boys and their father ate in the kitchen. The girls and their mother waited on the table and they ate after the men went back to the fields. With the three meals a day, Mrs. Lee and her daughters started at four o'clock in the morning and were done at nine o'clock at night. No modern conveniences were in the house such as electricity and running water. All the meals were cooked on a wood cook stove. The coffee was ground by hand, each day's meat was cut from a home butchered beef by hand and bread was baked twice a day.

The girls weeded the large garden and took care of the chickens and milked the cow. Mary also remembers driving derrick for stacking the hay.

Some neighbors were easy to get along with and others more difficult. There were always battles over water, fences, livestock and such. Frank McArthur and Bill Lee had their differences and at one time Frank put a post in the middle of the road and another at the side of the road with a chain between and a lock on the chain. He did not want the Lee family to leave their ranch. Frank felt he owned a portion of the ranch that Lee was buying. A fellow named Campbell owned the land joining the Lees and he let them through his property. The neighbors told the Lee's to go stay with the Parmee family overnight, (the present Lem Ernest ranch). During the night several of the neighbor men took the posts down. The idea was so that no one could say Bill Lee did it and so he would not know anything about it. The Lee family went home the next day and they never did say anything to the McArthurs about it and the McArthurs never said anything. Sometimes differences were settled in simple ways and other times more drastic steps had to be taken.

Mary remembers they always drove their horse and buggy to Fall City, (as her father always called Fall River Mills) to church every Sunday unless the weather was too bad.

The Lee children were growing up and were getting married. The girls were all married at the Lee ranch home.

Elbert married Claudia Payne, Wanda married Merton Callison, Blanch married Fred Taylor, Elmina married Meryl Whipple, Alice married Ellis Griffith, John married Elma Carpenter then Doris Pope,

W.H. Lee family, 1925. Back L. to R.: Elmina, John, Blanch, Wanda, Nora, Bill, Elbert. Front L. to R.: Alice, Mary, Lillian, William, Frank.

Mary married Willis Albaugh, Bill married Ada Reynolds, Nora never married, Frank married Vira Day then Erma was his second wife.

Elbert had gone into World War I and left home. As Bill and Lillian were getting older the reins of the ranch were turned over to John, Bill and Frank. Wanda, Elmina and Mary had all married ranchers in the Fall River Valley so were still close to home. Nora stayed at home for quite some time then went to Redding and worked for a farm advisor, Blanch married a farm advisor from Susanville, and Alice married a school principal. Alice was killed in 1948 in a tragic accident when a tree fell on her in a windstorm in Oregon.

After Alice's death Bill and Lillian were devastated and decided to give up the ranch. Bill would never let anyone play the piano again or mention Alice's name in his presence. Bill's eyesight was failing fast and he was going blind. Lillian had been crippled since childhood from an accident. She walked with a cane and it was hard for her to get around. Bill and Lillian were very private people and never told their business to anyone. Annabelle said, "you just did your work and never ask any questions".

John moved back into the large ranch house with Bill and Lillian with his two children Carma and Bobby. Bill Jr. lived on the ranch as did Frank. Bill's children all worked on the ranch as did the other grandchildren. There were several homes on this large ranch to accommodate the families.

After Lillian Lee was unable to cook for the hired men, Ada, Bill's wife did the cooking with the help of her daughters.

December 19, 1939 Mr. and Mrs. William H. Lee celebrated their fiftieth wedding anniversary at the home of their daughter Mrs. Willis Albaugh. All of their ten children were in attendance.

After the death of Alice her husband Ellis Griffith persuaded Bill Lee to form a corporation. In 1950 the W.H. Lee Company Inc. was formed and 88 year old Bill Lee retired. The Lee ranch was in the hands of the three brothers. John had always wanted to go to Canada and now he thought he would never have his chance. Frank and Bill were not sure they wanted this huge responsibility.

Annabelle married Jack Kelly and they went to work on the Lee ranch. Their main job was tending the cattle in the summer at Widow Valley and irrigating there. The herd of cattle began to dwindle as the Lee brothers sold some off.

Jack and Annabelle decided to leave the ranch and moved to Fall River where Jack went to work for P.G.&E.

Mary and Willis Albaugh at
his retirement from the
Fair Board, 1978

Bill and Lillian moved to old Shasta to a warmer climate for a short time then in January 1958 Bill Lee a prominent cattleman from the Fall River area for over sixty years passed away at 95 years of age.

Lillian Lee went to live with her four daughters, sharing her time among the four different homes. She also lived to the age of 95 when she passed away in November 1966.

In 1960 the W.H. Lee Company Inc. disbanded and the historic Lee ranch was sold to Spencer Murphy from San Francisco and Shingletown. Murphy also bought Widow Valley from Bill and John. John fulfilled a lifetime dream and moved to Canada. Frank went to work for Lorenz Lumber Company and Bill retired.

The thirty-five head of horses and seven hundred head of cattle were sold to Edison Faulk of Yreka. The Lee ranch was out of business. A legacy ended.

Murphy kept the ranch for fourteen years.

In 1974 David and Jo Rita Gates were looking for a ranch to buy. When they first found the Lee ranch Jo Rita fell in love with the massive old ranch house. Being raised on a farm in the mid west she knew when she saw the ample supply of water from springs on the ranch and the good soil that this was a valuable ranch. She had an immediate love affair with the ranch and knew this was the place for them.

With excellent help from Jim Utterback they were schooled in the ways of running a cattle ranch. Barns and homes were repaired and rebuilt. The mummified potatoes and onions were removed from the upstairs bedrooms and war was declared on the varmints. Workers moved in to restore the house and with the help of Mary Albaugh as she told Jo Rita how the house used to be when the Lee family lived there. The old house once more came to life as a home and is a beautiful reminder of the way it was when the Lees so lovingly cared for it. Annabelle remembers all of the beautiful hand knitted afghans that her grandmother had covering all of the furniture.

The Gates family at first only used the big house as their summer home and their foreman ran the ranch in their absence. But now they live there full time. They love their beautiful old home with the antiques, nostalgia, creaks and groans and even a friendly ghost.

The Lee family was sad to see their home ranch sold, but changes are made and life must go on. Only Mary, John and Nora are left of the children of Bill and Lily Lee. The twenty-four grandchildren and thirty-six great grandchildren that are the legacy of the Lee's can still be proud that even though the ranch now belongs to David and Jo Rita Gates, many old timers still call it the Lee ranch at the end of Lee Road just east of McArthur, Calif.

Glorianne Weigand
October 16, 1994

A Likely Story

Heritage and a big heart go hand in hand with a lot of things in this life, but nowhere is it more important than in the livestock industry.

Heritage is a fact that you were raised in the cattle industry and love it enough to fight to stay there. It isn't an easy life, but a gratifying way of living. You fight the weather, the water problems, drought, the government agencies, environmentalists, sick cows, calving problems and broken down machinery. You go through low cattle prices and sometimes it looks a little better so you stay in there, fighting to keep your ranch and family going.

A big heart is most important. You crawl out of a nice warm bed at 2 A.M. to go check the heifers that always seem to wait until nighttime in a snow blizzard to have calving problems. The worst problems always happen during the worst weather. You get that cranky heifer in and try to get a halter on her so you can pull the calf. She fights you and she is scared to death. This only makes matters worse. You finally get her under control and get the calf pulled. The calf is cold and you are cold, but you forget about yourself and start rubbing the calf dry and try to breath life into him. You forget how cold and miserable the weather is and you are just thankful that you found the heifer in time to save that newborn calf. This isn't only a big heart that makes you do this but a way of life. Your survival and how you love and take care of your cows and your land. In the snowy cold winters in Modoc County and the beautiful grassy hillsides and meadows in summer. This is your life, the land you love and care for, the animals you love and care for. These are all the things that have made Rob Flournoy the cattleman, good neighbor and friend to many that he is. These are the things Rob has been through as well as his father and his father before him. Now Rob's son Pearce is carrying on the tradition and the fourth generation of ranching as well as the rest of the Flournoy cousins of Likely, Calif. The descendants and cattlemen, great grandsons of John Flournoy who are still in the cattle industry are Pearce, Rodney, Bill, John and David.

A big man with an easy smile and a handshake for all is one of those rugged cattlemen with heritage and heart. Rob Flournoy from Likely, Modoc County, is known and admired by many. This man, a friend to all, entered life and the livestock industry May 14, 1919. His whopping birth weight was fourteen pounds and he claims to be the second largest

Rob Flournoy.

child born in Modoc. But as Rob says, "On one of them old spring scales, they could be off a little bit." Rob was the fifth son of Arthur Flournoy.

In 1881 Rob's grandfather, John Daniel Flournoy rode into the lush and unclaimed land of Modoc County. He came to start his ranch and raise his family. He had come from Missouri and came west with his family during the Civil War. Even though he was only nineteen years old he knew what he wanted and settled and claimed his ranch.

John returned to Yolo County to marry Frances Jackson and bring her 450 miles in a buggy to their new home in the wild lands of northern California. John and Frances had four sons, Arthur born in 1879, Will born in 1881, Eldon born in 1883 and Frank born in 1886.

It has been written many times that when in 1893 the gold field markets collapsed and the depression hit its peak John Flournoy was deep in debt and he was unable to meet his obligation. His banker was in Chico and had no idea how to manage a ranch in the rugged country of Modoc. The banker foreclosed and forced the Flournoys off of their ranch nearly penniless.

Not willing to be beaten, Mr. and Mrs. Flournoy filed a 640 acres homestead each on the Likely tablelands and moved their sons to the unfertile land. The land was unsuitable for most livestock so the ingenious Flournoy raised horses. The loan company tried to run the property that they had foreclosed on, and it took them less than a year to realize they

The Flournoy Gang. Back row, L. to R.: Brothers in birth order, Kenneth, John, Harry, Don, Rob, Warren. Front: their sons, Bill, John, David, Pearce, Craig, Rodney.

could not run a ranch and they begged John and Frances to return and reclaim their mortgage.

Mr. Flournoy's theory and lifetime philosophy was of asking no man to do what he wouldn't do himself. This is a belief that is carried through the Flournoy family today and they all work side by side with their hired help and each other doing anything and everything that is expected of a rancher.

John's sons grew up and started working on the ranch or in other enterprises. Arthur stayed on the ranch, Will married a Williamson girl and moved to the Williamson ranch. Eldon went into the store business and Frank went into the Hotel business.

Arthur was a telephone operator for the NCO Railroad at Likely and he would visit with an operator from Madeline named Lutie Long. The long distance romance started and soon Arthur was courting Lutie and they were married. Arthur moved his new bride to the home ranch where Bill Flournoy now lives. To this union ten children were born. Helen, Mabel, Hazel, Georgia, Kenneth, John, Harry, Don, Robert and Warren. All but two of the children were born at home on the ranch.

As the Flournoy sons grew up they all learned to work on the ranch and do all the things it took to be a cow man. A young man named Roy Swain was running the Jess Valley ranch and Kenneth was running the Likely ranch. When the young boys would misbehave they would be sent to Jess Valley for Roy to deal with. Rob loved the young cowboy Roy so much that he would go through "Hell and High Water" to be with him. He wanted to learn all he could from the young buckaroo and to this day Rob admires and loves Roy. "Oh, he wasn't easy on us," Rob would exclaim, "but he wanted to make men out of us." Roy could jerk you off of your horse and give you a dutch rub that Rob can still feel. If Roy sent us out to get a cow or calf and we came back without it or didn't tell the truth we knew we were in for it. He'd tell the boys, "the next time I send you out there I want you to do what you're told to do. If you're not man enough to live with us here in Jess Valley, go home." It was our pride that kept us there. We knew if we went home we'd get it again with a hickory switch. "Roy tried to raise us right."

Roy loves to tell the story of when he came riding in one day and smelled smoke coming from the barn. He knew those boys had been smoking in there. He hurried to get the fire out. That evening he told Rob and Don that if they wanted to smoke they could smoke with all the cowboys. Rob remembers getting so sick that he and Don ran to the creek and laid in the water. To this day neither Don nor Rob ever smoked.

Roy tells that Rob was kind and gentle with his horses and livestock. A good hand and a real good kid is what Roy says about Rob. He would do anything to please you is how Roy describes Rob.

The Flournoy kids went to school in Likely and when the older ones had to go to high school they moved to Alturas. There was no school bus and no way of getting to school so they moved to where the school was. In 1923 their home burned in Likely so it was inevitable they move to town.

Rob loved sports and played all of them extremely well. Basketball and football were his favorites. He was just one of the guys he says, "I never did anything special."

In 1943 Rob married Lizzette Pearce. She had lived in Susanville when she was younger. Her family moved to Alturas where her dad managed the Farmers Exchange. From this business venture JFG Motors was started and Mick Jones, Flournoys and Oscar Gustalison were the owners.

Rob and Lizzette have five children. Susan, Joanne, Pearce, Shelly and Craig and eight grandchildren.

Rodeo was an every day event on cattle ranches. With roping and doctoring cattle. Riding horses and breaking them. Rob was one of the ranchers along with Masten Ramsey to start the Likely Roping Clubs annual rodeo. It was just after the war and the guys decided to do something exciting. They felt a rodeo would be fun to do and add a little excitement for the small town of Likely. Around 1942 the ranchers built corrals, arena, bleachers and fences and started a rodeo that was held on the fourth of July for many years. Masten Ramsey and Rob were the arena directors, Harry was the announcer and Don and Warren were the pickup men. The Flournoys pretty well ran the show. The land was some of their land. They kept the bucking horses. They had about seventy-five bucking horses that were donated from many different ranchers. When the horses quit bucking they would be sold and the money given to the rancher that owned them, but in the meantime Rob took care of them and fed them. The Likely Roping Club put on rodeos in Alturas and Cedarville. They hauled their horses to Lakeview, Cedarville, McArthur, Susanville and Alturas.

The Likely Rodeo had to be changed to a weekend in June because they could not compete with the Klamath Falls and Reno rodeos on the Fourth of July. A lively dance was held in the Likely dance hall and the night would be filled with chants as the local Indians played their stick games. A good time was had by all and everyone was sad to see the Likely Rodeos end in the mid 60's. Rob said everyone wanted to go on to other things and the insurance got so high they just quit. They still had ropings and play days, but not a full fledged rodeo.

The Flournoy boys nor their sons ever competed in the rodeo. Rob said that people would think they would give their own the best stock or that they would be partial. He thought it was just best that they ran the show and not compete.

Rob never went to college. He wanted to go, but his dad told he and Don if they went to college he might as well sell the ranch and divide the money and that would be the end of it. Rob said that he and Don knew every fence corner on the ranch and hated to see it sold. In 1946 he and Don and Warren decided to buy it. Warren had gone to college in Sacramento. He was in the service in France and he got a French lawyer to help him out and the three of them bought their dad out. John had gone on to college in Reno and went into the stock and bond trade and was a

Rob Flournoy with the Modoc County Sheriffs Posse.

broker. Harry was in the store business. Kenneth had been in the service, but had a place of his own.

When Rob was a young man he played in a dance band called the Seven Knights of Rhythm. Their group consisted of Virgil Linto and Loren Ballard on the piano, Rob Flournoy and Arnold Hironomous on the saxophone and clarinet, Keith Smith, saxaphone, Koffman on the trumpet, K.C. Tierney on the trumpet. Bud Standfley on the tuba and string bass. Lt. Geyer on the trombone, and Chuck Hickerson and Jack Weldon on the drums. Their band was good and they had a contract to go to Hawaii to play on a cruise ship. They were just about ready to go when the war broke out and all their plans were forgotten.

The Flournoy brothers started working their sons into the ranch business. Today Pearce is running Rob's share of the ranch and Billy, John and David are running the share that their dad Don had. At one time when all the ranches were together they ran around 3,500 to 4,000 head of mainly Hereford cattle. Rob and Lizzette still live on the same place that Rob has lived on for sixty years.

When the U.S. Forest Service started talking about cutting range rights Rob decided to buy the Willow Creek ranch and run his cattle there. He also leased all of the Weyerhauser property in that area. It is a seventy-five mile trip to truck the cattle from Likely to Willow Creek. The Warner range and the Bureau of Land Management range on the Madeline Plains are still the lands that Pearce and Rob run their cattle on. Range improvements have been an important part of their success story. Weyerhauser Lumber Company planted many trees and they like the cattle to range it to eat the competitive grasses that starve the small trees from water. The cattle are moved at intervals so the lands are not overgrazed. In the early spring the cattle are turned on to the table lands between Likely and Alturas. The first of July they move to the Warner range then to the Forest Service at Jess Valley. Pearce runs between 700 and 800 head of cattle and this is a full time job for any man.

One thing that Rob enjoys very much is the Modoc Tribe Ride. This event is in its fifty-third year. The Tribe Ride was started one day when during a Rotary meeting it was mentioned that the Forest Service was going to cut the range permits in a certain area. This meant a cut in personnel in the Forest Service and a cut in the people that the ranchers helped support. It would mean a cut at the machinery businesses, the gas plants, the grocery stores, feed stores and clothing stores. The town of Alturas couldn't stand the loss in revenue. The businessmen decided it would be a good idea to go out on the range and take a look at the situation and see for themselves just why the Forest Service needed to make these cuts. The Forest Supervisor said if they could get some horses gathered for people to ride they would go make a study. The ones that couldn't ride went in a truck. Cooks were brought in from the Forest Service line camps or the Sheriff would bring them from the jail. They went to the Warner range and rode to Patterson Mill, Pepperdine Camp and Mill Creek. Bleachers were brought out and they would sit and have speakers and lectures, learning about the range conditions. This began to be an annual event and everyone looked forward to it.

It has always been held the third week in August. Men travel a long way to take part in the ride and the companionship. You have to be invited to go on the ride and the member that sponsors you is responsible for you.

Rob didn't get to go on the earliest rides because he was at home putting up loose hay. It wasn't until they started baling hay and had the bales to haul for the horses on the tribe ride to eat that Rob got to go.

Rob loves to go to Idaho every year to elk hunt. He has bagged a few big Modoc buck deer in his time.

Rob's retirement hobby is what he calls Harvey Creek. It is his and Lizzette's hideaway where they love to be. As you travel toward Blue Lake after leaving Jess Valley you come close to their haven. The criteria for a building to be placed there is it has to be one hundred years old, hand made with square nails and no paint. The little settlement consists of the old Alturas Jail, the Doris log home, the Everly cabin, the Fitzhugh cabin and a two story outhouse. Life is very comfortable there. They have gravity-flow water, electricity and satellite T.V. Rob said he would rather be there than anywhere else.

Rob has done his share of traveling nationwide and many times to Washington D.C. with his responsibilities of Cattlemen and many other organizations. His list of what he has been involved in would stagger most any man, but Rob has done them all and done them well. His lists of achievements and committees are Past President, California Cattlemen's; Director, American National Cattlemens; Local, State and National BLM boards; member, State Board of Forestry; Chairman, Modoc Forestry Board; Director, Shasta Cascade Wonderland Association; Member, Modoc, Los Angeles and California Chamber of Commerce; Past President, Modoc Chamber of Commerce; Member and Past Captain, Modoc County Sheriff Posse; Charter Member, B.P.O.E. 1756; 1981 President, Alturas Rotary Club; Director, Sonoma County Trail Blazers; Director, Rancheros Visitadores; Director, Vice President, President and Committeeman for CCA Public Lands committee and Hide and Brand Committee; Director and Committeeman, ANCA Forest and Public Lands and Brand and Theft; Chairman, BLM Susanville District Advisory Board; Member, School Board; Fire Commissioner, South Fork District; President Modoc Council of Natural Resources; Member, Superior Court Juvenile Advi-

Top, L. to R.: Shelly, Craig, Joanne, Pearce, Susan. Front: Lizzette and Rob.

sory Committee; Director, Modoc Council Boy Scouts of America Honorary Member, Future Farmers of America; Livestock Man of the Year State of California 1980; Organized Ducks Unlimited of Modoc County; Modoc County Secret Witness; Livestock Man of the Year Modoc County 1983.

Rob is trying to slow down a bit and let the younger generation step in to fill his boots. But they are pretty big and busy boots to fill, so it may take a whole herd of young ones to keep up with his list of committees and accomplishments.

When Rob was asked about his plans for the future he said he just wanted to throw another log on the fire and enjoy himself.

Glorianne Weigand
December 21, 1994

A Cowboy's Life

"I was riding this ole owl-headed horse and he didn't know a durn thing. Jeff Eades and I were going to corral some cows at the Dixie Valley ranch and I wanted to shut the gate at the end of the corral. I went galloping down the corral and as I passed the barn that dumb son-of-a-gun ducked into the open door of the horse barn. When he hit that board floor at a full run he lost his footing and went a scrambling. I went a flying through the air and lit in the manger. I never even skinned a knuckle, but I sure wasn't very happy. That horse never had a brain in his head and he never got any smarter."

That was only one of the wrecks that Forest Carpenter can tell you about in his lifetime of being a buckaroo. Forest is one of the Carpenter brothers that are well known in the horse world and ranch life of Northern California and Southern Oregon.

Forest was the eighth child born to Winfred (Bill) and Lovie Carpenter. Winfred had come across the plains from Missouri with his parents and twin brother and the rest of the family when he was only a baby. Forest's grandparents with their six boys and seven girls settled near New Plymouth, Idaho. When Winfred grew up and met Lovie, they married and started a family of their own.

The large family were a close and happy bunch. Twelve children were born to Bill and Lovie, four girls and eight boys. It seemed to be the nature of the family to give most everyone a nickname as Winfred himself was known as Bill. Not many people would even recognize the real name of most of the boys. The oldest was Buck (Lloyd), Minnie Ellen, Spike (Elton), Hude (Hugh), Loren, Wad (Harold), Bob (Robert), Forest, Lin, Nel, Pauline and Inez.

Forest, their eighth child, was born June 6, 1919 in Gooding, Idaho. One of his earliest recollections is when the family moved from Gooding, Idaho to Fall River Valley in Northern California. It was the summer of 1926. Forest can remember celebrating his seventh birthday while they were on their month long journey. They started out in May so they could get to Fall River for the haying season.

Bill and Lovie had a ranch rented in Vale, Oregon before that. Bill's brother Bob had moved to the Fall River Valley and had written to Bill and told him what a wonderful place it was. Bill and Lovie decided to move their family to California.

The family had an old hay wagon they fixed up with a tarp over the top and had a cook stove in it and a bed. You might say one of the first camp trailers. Another wagon carried their belongings. They drove two teams, Buck and Spike were the teamsters. They also had an old Maxwell car. They had some saddle horses and drove a bunch of loose horses and a bunch of milk cows. They would camp out each night sleeping on the ground. Bill, Lovie and the youngest kids would share the bed in the cook wagon. The cows had to be milked night and morning and the family would pack up and be on their way. Forest was young and can't remember

Back Row L. to R.: Lin, Spike, Bob, Forest, Wad. 2nd Row: Inez, Pauline, Minnie, Nel, Orville Cessna. Front: Myrtle Cessna, Bill, Lovie, Harold Cessna, Wendall. Babies are twins Myrna and Myra.

a lot of particulars about the trip. He just knows it was an exciting time, moving to a new land, and quite a way to celebrate a birthday.

Uncle Bob's ranch was next to the Lee ranch near McArthur. He had an extra house, so they moved there to live. Later they found a place of their own.

The Carpenter kids started to school at the Pine Grove school. Forest was in the second grade and Zereda Jentzen was the school teacher. There were about twenty kids in the school. Some of them were Frank Lee, Jay Cessna, Art Cessna, Ola Cupp, Bud Cupp and Art Christensen. Uncle Bob's children Don, Robert, Davie, Kenneth, Elma and Lenora also went there. Just Hude, Loren, Wad, Bob and Forest went to school there at that time. The others were either too old or too young.

Before long Bill Carpenter found a place near Pittville and moved his family over there. The kids then went to the Rocky Comfort school near Little Valley. After a time they moved to Glenburn, but didn't stay there to long then they moved back to Pittville. Forest finished the eighth grade there at the Rocky Comfort school and that ended his official school career. From then on he learned by doing and working and living.

Forest's first job was at the age of eight when he started driving derrick and stacking hay for his dad. Bill had a hay contracting business. With all of those boys he may as well do something that would keep them busy and help to feed the family. Most of the hay contracts that Bill had was only to haul it and stack it. He also did custom farming.

Forest can remember that when they worked in the salt grass hay for Andrew McWilliams that his feet got so sore he couldn't even walk. He had no shoes and walking in the salt grass was like walking on a million little needles. The grass was fine and stickery and cut and pierced his little feet until they bled. His Dad finally had to buy some shoes for him.

The Carpenter family put up the hay for McWilliams, Cale Guthrie and Aub Burton. Forest drove the big derricks. He thought that old derrick horse had the hardest mouth ever. He would pull and pull with all his might to get that old mare to back up. He finally learned how to handle her. Buck and Spike pitched the hay on to the wagons. Hude, Loren, Wad and Bob drove the wagons. Bill Carpenter got $1.25 a ton for a short haul of alfalfa and $1.50 a ton for a long haul of a mile or so. The grass hay was harder to handle and they were paid $1.75 a ton. Bill and the older boys took turns at stacking. They started their haying contracting business as soon as school was out and finished when school started. It was a long hard summer for the Carpenter boys with not much fun.

Forest broke his first horse at the age of fifteen, and he just about spoiled her. She was a filly that his brother-in-law Harold Vestal had given him. One of the best horses that Forest had of his Dad's to break was a catch colt from one of the work mares and one of Bill Hollenbeaks studs down on the Pit River. Forest broke quite a few horses until he went into the Army. The early years of breaking horses seemed to set the pattern for his life's work.

The Carpenter brothers and sisters started to go their own way and marry or go into the Army. Buck married Lottie Campbell, Ellen married Orville Cessna, Spike married Wilba Day, Hude married Ivadel Day, Forest married Marjorie Taylor, Lin married Jessie Emerick, Nel married Chris Emerick, Pauline married Harold Vestal. Loren, Wad, Bob and Inez never married.

Forest went into the Army in 1942 when he was twenty-three years old. He was in Texas six months, he then went to England, Germany, Normandy, France and Holland. He was in for a three year hitch and says he never saw a thing over there that I would ever want to go back again for.

Before Forest went into the Army he was working for Jess Eldridge and when he came home three years later Jess was holding his job for him. It was as if he never left. Jess was a great guy to work for and had really good horses. The food was great and you couldn't have asked for a better place to be. The going rate for a buckaroo before Forest went into the Army was $50.00 a month.

Forest and his brother Wad wanted to see some new country and they headed to Paisley, Oregon and went to work for the ZX ranch. By that time a buckaroo was paid $175.00 a month. This was 1950 and they loved the buckaroo life of going out on the desert with the cattle and sleeping in tents and eating lots of beef and beans at the chuck wagon. You had no worries, just follow those old cows and move them from place to place.

In the winters the brothers would come back to California near Bella Vista where the weather was a little better and break horses all winter. Then when spring hit and it was time to move the ZX cows to the desert they would head back to Oregon.

Probably the biggest place and Forest's most favorite place was the ZX. You went out in the spring with the cattle and the chuck wagon, and home in the fall. You didn't set around the bunkhouse. You were moving cattle around all the time. They would move the cattle to Sycan Valley. It was a huge meadow. It took five days to drive the cattle there. It was a huge swamp west of Summer Lake. They drove 6,500 head of dry cows and the next year they drove 8,500 out there. That would be about the first of April and the cows would calve out on the desert. The calves weren't branded or handled until they came home in the fall. The ZX cattle were mainly Hereford and a little Durham cross. "No blacks in

Verl Wysong, Loren Carpenter, Paul Rutherford, Cougar Beal, Cactus Smyth, Clevon Dixon. After calf branding at Alvord Ranch, 1953.

Back: Wad, Lin, Forest, Bob.
Front: Loren, Hugh, Spike, Buck, Lovie, Bill, Nell, Pauline, Inez.

those cattle", declared Forest. The bulls had to be driven out to the cows and they would drive 500 head of bulls to meet up with the cow herd.

One time the ZX chuckwagon that was on an old truck broke through a bridge when they were trying to cross a creek. They had quite a time hauling it out of there and setting things right again.

The second year on the job at the ZX when the Carpenter Brothers came back Forest broke his leg. It was the first day on the job in March. About two hours after he started to work, his horse fell on him and broke his leg. Forest went back to McArthur and stayed with his folks until he could get a walking cast on his leg and get around. He had the cast on until the Fourth of July. He then went to Big Valley and went back into the hay field where he drove a team on a mowing machine for Lee Crews.

In 1965 Forest went to the MC ranch at Adel, Oregon and worked for Clevon Dixon who was Cow Boss there. Again Forest loved the times out on the wagon in the desert riding herd on the cattle. They had a good cook while there and he was quite an old character. He had been an old cowboy down in Arizona, but got too stove up for the cowboy life so he just became a camp cook. You would walk up to the tent where he was cooking and the old guy would be talking to himself and even answering himself. Carrying on quite a conversation.

There would be about twelve cowboys and the cook out with the wagon. Each cowboy had about seven horses in each of their strings, but only kept three with them. Each cowboy was responsible for keeping his own horses shod.

While in the Oregon Country with the MC Forest was at the Coleman ranch also. Loren Carpenter put in some time at the Alvord ranch. Forest and his wife Marjorie who he married in 1956 spent their summers at the Coleman. Forest cowboyed and Marjorie did the cooking. There they ran a lot of horses on the desert like wild horses and gathered them in the Fall to pick out the ones they wanted to break. Some winters Forest broke quite a few horses. One winter he broke as many as fifteen horses. That is the most he ever started in one winter.

Forest had a chance to be cow boss on one outfit. His wife was cooking on this ranch. She thought it would be a good job for Forest and they would settle in one place, but he just thought it would be a lot of headaches. And would rather just be a buckaroo. The cowboy blood ran in his veins and he didn't like staying in one place too long.

Forest worked on the Dixie Valley ranch in Lassen County in North Eastern California for several years. While he worked there Bill Spalding was the manager and Tom Connolly owned it. Jeff Eades was a half breed Indian that worked on the ranch and he and his wife Martha had a cabin of their own not far from the main two story house where Bill and his wife Hazel lived. The main dining room was in the big house and at the time Forest worked there, Selana LaMarr an Indian lady was the cook. Her husband Lymann Lymarr was the chore boy and handy man.

Others that lived and worked there were Forest's brother Wad, Lee Crews and his wife Avis, Nelmer Spalding, (Bill's son), Byrel Wendt, Arthur Barnes and Iverson Barnes. Hack Lambert worked there part of the time when the cattle needed to be worked or they needed extra help.

The long table with its white oil cloth covering was always set for twenty men or more. The dishes were placed upside down along each side after they were washed after each meal. Just in case someone extra would show up for a meal or an extra cowboy came riding by, Hazel Spalding wanted to be sure they would feel welcome to set down to a meal and a place had already been set for them.

The Dixie Valley Ranch was a beautiful ranch, set in a valley of meadows. Eight miles from Little Valley it was like a little world of its own. Cowboys, cows, good horses and a whole way of life. Jeff Eades could be seen sitting on his porch on a summer evening working on his rawhide braiding or teaching some of the young cowboys like Lee Crews to do silver work. The other cowboys sat around swapping their stories or cleaning their tack or just resting after a long days ride. The hay crew was a very important part of the ranch. Forest and Wad broke work horses on the mowing machines in the summer time.

Forest remembers Jeff Eades, the well loved half breed Indian from Dixie Valley as one of the best cowhands he ever ran across. "Jeff was a real fair hand with a rawhide rope. He used a sixty foot riata and handled it with ease. One time Jeff roped a wild, bucking, bawling yearling steer. His cinch was a hanging loose an inch or so, but that didn't bother Jeff none. He just threw his loop, and caught that big ole steer. His dallies were a runnin and the smoke boiling off of his saddle horn. Ole Jeff just sat right down on that ole saddle, hung tight and stopped that ole steer. Never bothered that ole cowboy a bit and he was in his late sixties then. Quite a buckaroo, that Jeff Eades".

One time the Dixie crew went down to Red Bluff to the Connolly ranch there to ship some cattle. Forest was riding a young horse and he blew up and went to bucking. Jeff rode into Forest's bucking horse to stop it and Jeff's horse started to buck harder than Forest's. Jeff just took his romal and over and undered his ole horse with every jump, and he finally got things under control. Jeff never lost a stirrup or his hat and again, it never bothered Jeff in the least.

At one time Jeff told Hack Lambert that he wished he were forty years younger so he could ride colts, but from the stories that Forest tells, age didn't bother Jeff too much.

When Forest was asked if he had any real wrecks with his broncs, he laughed and said he had his share. Some were bad and some were pretty stupid.

Lee and Forest were breaking some horses one time and Forest had a snaffle bit horse with a bozal on him. He wanted to teach that horse to watch a calf, he ran the rope through the bozal and roped the big fall calf. The calf went through the loop and caught a hind foot. The calf went one way and the horse went the other and Forest landed about thirty feet ahead. He said it never taught the horse a durn thing, but Forest sure got a lesson. "Never hurt me a bit, I just rolled like a punkin", is the way the seasoned cowboy puts it.

While at Dixie, Nelmer, Hack, Forest, Wad and Bill corralled about twenty-five or thirty wild horses off of the B.L.M. They had rounded them up and taken them to the main corrals at the ranch. They found them up near Coyote Reservoir and worked them easy and got them to the ranch. Bill wanted to look them over. There were some real pretty horses in the bunch and a pretty rank stud. After they had inspected them, Bill decided to take them back the way they came and turn them into a feed yard. They could have gone through a stack yard, but they were pretty sure of themselves and didn't think they would have any trouble. They headed the horses out the gate thinking they were in control, but when they got away from the corrals, the wild mustangs with the big stallion in the lead took off like a shot and dodged the cowboys like wild bullets. They couldn't even keep up with their dust. They lost them all and never ever got that many of them corralled again. This is one of Forest's memorable times and he is the only one left of those five cowboys to tell the story.

Forest was out with a new horse in the corral. His first time on him and the horse was bucking so hard that he fell on his side, with Forests leg underneath him. Bill Spalding was watching the action and when Forest picked himself up off the ground he told Bill, "I don't believe I can ride that horse outside". Bill said, "Oh yes you can, get back on". Forest got back on the horse and out he went. The horse had the air knocked out of him when he hit the ground.

It must have taught him a lesson as he never bucked with Forest again. Wad had rode the colt the year before and he bucked with Wad every time he got on him.

"One thing about Bill Spalding," declared Forest, "he always believed in his cowboys and gave them lots of encouragement, a wonderful guy to work for."

In 1950 when Wad and Forest were at Little Valley at one of the rodeos, someone bet Forest a drink that he could not ride his young colt into Ned Bognuda's Empty Holster Bar. They opened the door and Forest rode in. The floor sagged, Forest took his beer, but said the ceiling was so low he could hardly tip his head back for a drink. Wad opened the door and Forest rode his horse out. He'd won that bet.

Most of the Dixie Valley cattle were shipped south for the winter. Forest and Wad spent their winters breaking colts.

One time Connolly bought a bunch of horses out of Nevada from Harry Wilson. They brought them back to Dixie, but some of them scattered and headed back to Nevada. Forest and Hack Lambert had to go to Ash Valley east of Adin to retrieve one of them. It had gotten that far and had come in with the work horses at the Bath ranch during haying. Hack and Forest went after it and it was so mean and hard to load they had to pull it into the truck with one of Bath's teams. The next day Forest saddled him up and started to ride him. He was just another colt to break.

In May of 1955 Bill and Hazel Spalding left Dixie Valley after twelve years. Their son Nelmer quit the Connolly ranch at Big Valley. Tom Connolly was spending a lot of time in court and didn't have time for the ranch. Forest and Wad Carpenter stayed on to ride for the cows and Selena LaMarr cooked and Byrel Wendt was the mechanic. It was just a skeleton crew. The Carpenter brothers gathered and branded. The work went on. In June Tom Connolly sent Joe DeMello, an old rodeo cowboy to manage the ranch. He had no idea how to run such a vast enterprise. Forest and Wad and Selena had left in the three short months that DeMello ran Dixie Valley into the ground.

Forest went on to other jobs and he was kind of glad he did. He had broke fifteen horses the last winter that he was at Dixie Valley, and they were all really good, well bred horses. Connolly had bought a quarter horse-thoroughbred cross stud horse that was a rank son-of-a-gun. The colts were coming three year olds and Forest wasn't sure he wanted to tackle some of them. Most of them were ornery like the old stud horse. In 1958 to keep up the Carpenter tradition, another member of the family, Forest's brother Spike's son Wendall went to work for Dixie Valley to ride colts and cowboy. Forest said those colts were dirty cranky sons a guns. They had a lot of fire to them and were in Wendall's hip pocket most of the time.

When asked if he did any rodeoing, Forest commented that he had rodeoed just long enough to find out that was a tough way to make a living. A saddle bronc that he was riding threw him off onto his back. For twenty years Forest couldn't sit in a chair without hurting. It didn't bother him to ride a horse. Twenty years later while at the ZX in Paisley, Oregon a horse bucked into the fence and Forest got a foot hung up in the stirrup. Forest was trying to get away from him as he thought the

Richard Hart and Forest Carpenter, 1972.

Forest Carpenter.

horse was coming over backwards. When the horse jumped, Forest went over the saddle horn and landed on his chest. A severe pain hit him in the back and after that it never bothered him again. He said he must have had a rib out of place and this ordeal must have popped it back in place.

Forest moved from ranch to ranch and never had to look hard for a job. He worked on the Bidwell Ranch at Hat Creek for a time. The Trinity ranch in the Bald Hills out of Redding. There, the corral was so big that they broke horses in that you had to run them round and round to tire them out before you could ever do anything with them.

The cowboy's life was the life Forest wanted and he worked many places. Where there were horses to be rode or roping and branding or cattle to move is where you found Forest and usually his brother Wad. They were quite a pair.

The Trinity Alps is where Forest worked on an outfit where he had to pack in fifteen miles to the cow camp. All of your gear and grub had to be taken in by pack horse. It was a beautiful and peaceful place to be.

Forest's wife Marjorie passed away in 1983. They were living at Cottonwood at the time where he was doing day work on different ranches. He had four step children, Les, Betty, Charlotte and Roselee. Les and Betty have passed away. One daughter Charlotte married Don Hill from Cedarville. Don was cow boss on the MC Ranch for a time after Forest was there. They now live in Warner Valley out of Lakeview, Oregon. Roselee lives at Cloverdale, Idaho.

Forest went back to the C2 Ranch at Eagle Point, Oregon and worked there for a while. He then went back to the Lakeview area and did day work on several different ranches around there and Warner Valley and Drews Valley. Forest still does day work in the spring and Fall for O'Keefe, Lane and Hickey in Warner Valley. Even at the age of 76 Forest keeps working at the life he loves. He lives at Lakeview not far from his step daughter and son-in-law.

Of the twelve brothers and sisters of the Carpenter family, only Forest, Lin, Pauline and Inez are still living.

Fall River Valley is home to many of the ancestors of Bob and Bill Carpenter, who came from Idaho to a land they only heard about. They built their dreams and their families there.

The Carpenter boys are sure to be written in the "Legend Book of Buckaroos".

Glorianne Weigand
January 14, 1995

Proud to Be an American

"When a man can stand on his own land in the middle of a field of waving grain or grass and know that he is responsible for that grass, then he has achieved the greatest satisfaction that life has to offer". These were the words that 93 year old Kasper Weigand spoke many times, and he meant every word of it. "The country, the land and the people have been good to me. I wouldn't change it one bit if I had the chance to do it over again." Mr. Weigand carried a whopping big load of love for a country he adopted for his own when he was thirteen years of age. Young Kasper was born in the village of Salz on the Salle River north of Bavaria, Germany on February 2, 1870. His Father Kasper Weigand died of Typhoid fever when young Kasper was two years old. His mother Magdalena died when he was six years old. Young Kasper was moved about to many foster homes. Life was so poor in Germany that young Kasper was sent out to gather every goose feather that the geese would drop in the farm yards. They were gathered to sell or to make pillows to sell. Life was hard for the young boy and in his later years he never wanted to return to his homeland and he only had sad memories of his life there. Finally Kasper went to live with a half sister that he hardly knew. She had a son George Kirchner that became a dear friend to Kasper.

In 1883, two half brothers in Chicago in the U.S.A. provided passage and a small amount of money for Kasper to join them in the United States. One brother was a butcher and the other was a farmer.

Kasper was quite a scamp at that time. Aboard ship he used up all his money on candy and cigars and by the time he landed in America he didn't have a penny. The cigars made him so sick, that at the tender age of thirteen he gave up smoking. He was a penniless immigrant from Germany and scared to death.

Kasper got pretty hungry in Philadelphia waiting for the train to Chicago. He couldn't speak a word of English to ask anyone for some food. On the train he saddled up to an older lady with a big box of food

The family of
Kasper and Etta
Weigand, 1908.
Back: Pearl
and Clara.
Front: Kasper,
Etta and
Lawrence.

and she fed him all the way to Chicago. From that time on Kasper claimed that life in the United States was easy for him.

In Chicago his brothers tried to send him to school to learn to read and write English. They put him in the first grade and every time the children went out to play, he went home as he thought school was out. After about three months of that his brothers decided he had better get to work. That was the end of Kasper's education. He did manage to complete the third grade.

After two years Kasper was tired of the big city and drifted off to Missouri. He located near Maysville, and began life as a farmer.

Kasper met a young girl in Maysville that took his eye. Etta Wolf who was born in 1875 to a prominent farming family and Kasper were married March 21, 1893. The young couple started their farming career and their family. Daughter Clara was born in 1894, Pearl in 1896, Lawrence in 1899. A second son Ralph was born in 1904, but died at the age of two months from Whooping cough.

By 1909 Kasper had heard glowing accounts of life in the West. Adventure was in his blood and the town of Lakeview, Oregon was a place he thought he would like to farm. The family packed up their belongings and boarded the train to Reno, Nevada, then on to Alturas, California. Modoc County seemed quite unsettled and primitive compared to Missouri. The family found a place on Pine Creek to rent. They stayed there for a year and made hay and sold it to a livery stable at Alturas.

Kasper's nephew George Kirchner had also migrated to the United States and came west with the family. He was raised along with the Weigand children like a child of their own. The Weigand family never did go on to Lakeview as they had planned.

At Alturas Kasper rented a ranch from Sam Baty. Sam had a large Library and Kasper read all the books he could. George went to work for Sam Baty on the Corporation Ranch in Likely. When Sam Baty went to Adel, Oregon to manage the MC Ranch George also went to the MC and worked there for many years. George was drafted into World War I and received injuries in the service. He returned to the MC and stayed on there until his retirement.

In 1910 Mr. Weigand decided to look around the country a little more, so he moved his family to San Jose, California and bought a prune orchard. The first year it froze and he only got one box of prunes. Kasper worked in the brick yard to be able to feed his family. Etta, Clara, Pearl and Lawrence cut apricots to be dried. They were paid by the box. Clara finished grammar school while at San Jose.

The next year Kasper had so much fruit that he had to prop the limbs up to keep them from breaking. The Weigands decided this was a good time to sell out as they really didn't like the orchard business.

The winter of 1911 and 1912 found the family on the move again when they boarded the train to Wenatche, Washington. They moved on to Colville, Washington to do some farming. Here they were joined by cousins from Missouri, the Charlie Leonard family. Kasper rented a fertile farm near Arden, Washington, there he reaped a good return of crops for his hard labor. Land values were too high there for him to purchase a farm in Washington. Kasper had in his mind that he wanted to raise livestock. Again the Weigand family and the Leonards boarded the train to Susanville, California. Mr. Weigand had talked to some men that were in Susanville from Bieber. They told them that Big Valley was an up and coming place. Mr. and Mrs. Weigand left their children with the Leonards and boarded a stage coach to Bieber. They liked what they saw and sent for Clara, Pearl and Lawrence. The three young Weigands rode the stage coach to Hayden Hill where they spent the night in the hotel there. They then traveled on the next day to Bieber. The Leonards soon followed and the two families rented a two story house in Bieber that is still a dwelling there.

Kasper was told of a ranch on Willow Creek that may be for sale. The ranch had been owned by Andrew Gregg. The original homestead was patented to O.L. Stanley March 1873, 160 acres. Osias O. Stanley, 1873, 160 acres. and Agustas C. Herrick in 1875 160 acres. Andy Gregg bought the 480 acres of homesteads in 1891 for $2,000.00.

The Andy Gregg ranch was at one time part of Siskiyou County. In 1874 the State Legislature sliced off a part of Siskiyou County and formed Modoc County. At the lower end of the ranch was a marker that still said it was the corner of Siskiyou County.

Andy Gregg had been a bachelor and died at a young age from a scratch on his thumb that turned into blood poisoning. The ranch was going through legal proceedings with Andy's brothers. In the spring of 1913 Kasper drove his team from Bieber to inspect the ranch. As he drove over the knoll and looked over the meadow, he saw timothy that was as high as the horses back. He knew this was the place for him. The ranch was two and a half miles from Adin and had a log home on it. The cabin was in pretty sad shape. It was fine for a bachelor, but Etta was not too thrilled with it. Lawrence could remember the first time he saw his new home. He drove his team over the knoll and the black birds were thick in the spring sunshine and their songs filled the air.

Kasper paid $2,500.00 cash to the heirs of Andy Gregg and moved his family in to their new home. They had a team of horses, and three cows. One cow was red, one cow was black and one cow was white. This was the start for the herd of cattle that the industrious young man from Germany would soon have. He bought cattle and kept all of his heifers and soon nearly three hundred head of cows would be branded with the WK brand.

Pearl was in high school and she went to Adin to school. Lawrence went to grade school at the Center School District a few miles down the road. Mr. McKenzie was his teacher. Lawrence always had to fight the boys in each new school he came to. He had gone to so many different schools that he felt he had to prove himself as he was always picked on.

In 1914 Kasper started hauling lumber from the Conklin sawmill on Adin Mountain by team and wagon to build a new home. John Kresge was the master builder and by 1915 the family settled in to their new home.

In 1916 Mrs. Weigand and Clara took a trip to Missouri to visit Mrs. Weigand's ailing mother. While there, Clara received a letter from Pearl, that a young man from Stone Coal Valley, Phillip Miller had come to buy hay. When Clara returned home, she and Phillip dated a few times and were married. They divided their time between the Stone Coal ranch and the Andy Bean ranch near Bieber that they had bought. Their children, Dorotha who was born in 1918 and Alden who was born in 1929 went to the Washington School that was close to their ranch.

In 1919 Pearl married Andy Knudsen. They moved to Ash Valley where they rented the Perkins place for several years. They then moved back to the Watson place near Bieber that Kasper was renting. Their son Virgil was born in 1926. When Virgil started to school he also went to the Washington school with his cousins, Alden and Dorotha.

September 25, 1927 Lawrence married Norma Studley a girl from the neighboring ranch. They were married on the 101 Ranch at her parents home. Kasper and Etta turned the ranch over to Lawrence and were anxious to take a trip to Missouri to visit relatives. They spent quite some time there then came home and stayed one winter with Lawrence and Norma. Kasper had bought the Hugh Watson ranch near Bieber. (Presently owned by the Department of Fish and Game.) Pearl and Andy lived in one of the homes there, but there was a second house so Kasper and Etta moved into it. Before long Pearl and Andy moved to the Knight place which is now owned by Frosty Acres Ranch.

Lawrence and Norma started a family of their own. Avis was born in 1928, Cleo in 1930, Stan in 1933 and Dale in 1939.

Ranch life was busy and the two ranches were run together. Kasper was getting on in years and was slowing down quite a bit. When he was

Lawrence and Norma (Studley) Weigand
married Sept. 25, 1927.

eighty years old he said after all day on a horse he got pretty stove up, so he gave up riding.

In 1931 a young cowboy from the Fresno area came to Adin looking for work. His name was John Poytress and he and a friend had driven their old Model A Ford up north and wanted to be cowboys. It was June and most of the cattle were out on the range, and it was time to start haying.

John and his friend stopped at the Weigand ranch to look for work. Lawrence and Jim Elzea were out at Hayden Hill gathering the work horses from their spring range to bring them home for haying. John was hired on the next morning and drifted in and out of Big Valley for seven years working on the Weigand ranch each haying season. John finally got his wish and got to be a cowboy. He stayed on a little longer each year and helped with the fall riding. In 1936 John brought his girl friend up with him and they went to Reno and got married. John helped put up the hay and his new bride Marjorie helped Norma do the cooking for the hay crew. John and Marjorie then went back to Fresno. In 1942, Norma's father, Frank Studley asked John to come back to Big Valley and run his ranch.

John can tell many stories of the times he and Lawrence rode together and the different experiences he had with the Weigand family. When John was young he slept in the bunk house with five or six other young men at the Weigand ranch. John drove many colts to break them to mow or rake the hay. Bart and Barnie were a couple of his favorite colts and Daisy and Nellie were a couple good old mares.

At haying time when Lawrence needed to find a hay crew, he and his young son Stan would go down to Bieber along the river to the Ho-Bo jungle. Stan tells how it was kind of scary going in there. There would be smoke everywhere from their little camp fires. They would be cooking their dinner in cans over the fire and have a can of coffee boiling. They would wash their clothes in the Pit River and have them hanging on the willows to dry. They would have their bottles of liquor in their hands. Lawrence would ask if any of them knew how to work a team of horses. Sometimes there would be the same men he had the year before. They never went by their real names, and there was never a last name. Blackie, Slim, Cotton and Red were some that worked at the ranch from year to year. Some of the Ho-Bo's were also at the round house at the railroad at Nubieber. Stan tell's how the railroad cars would be lined with men laying on top of them, waiting for their next ride to the next town.

Red and Cotton came for several years and Cleo describes them as looking like a couple of the Seven Dwarfs, on payday Lawrence had to go to the bank so he could pay them in cash.

Different ones that worked had different talents. Dan Russell was a silver smith and made excellent bridles and did leather work. He had been a cook at the Dixie Valley Ranch at one time. Mr. Woodard drove his old car up from the Sacramento valley each year to work in the hay fields for Lawrence. He was a faithful hay hand and came back for many years.

The bunk house was a busy place in the summer, but maybe only one man would be there in the winter. Each spring Lawrence and Norma would empty the old straw out of the mattresses, wash the covers and fill them with clean straw. A table, a couple chairs, wash pan and lava soap, a lamp and along with the six cots made up the summer home of this hay crew. Breakfast was served in the house at six A.M., lunch at noon and supper at six P.M.

The cook was responsible for cooking the meals and Norma took care of the garden and baked the bread and made the butter. Besides Marjorie Poytress, some of the cooks were Alice Kiaser, Mrs. Sebright, Grace Hatfield, Devona Wolter and Grace Bath cooked there.

Three large stacks were put up on Lawrence's place. Along with the men they hired, Avis drove buck rake and Cleo and Stan drove derrick. One day the man on the hay stack waved at Cleo and she waved back. It was a windy day and the wind caught the derrick net swinging it around and broke the derrick pole. The whole haying operation had to be shut down while they went to the hills to cut a new derrick pole. Cleo said her dad didn't even yell at her.

After the hay was put up at the home ranch the whole crew and all the equipment was moved down to put the hay up on Kasper's place. The teams pulled the rakes the six miles down the road and the mowing machines were loaded on the hay rack wagons and the parade moved on down the road. The cook would go down there and do the noon meal cooking or the meal was sent down. The men would return in the evening and breakfast and supper were eaten at the home ranch.

It was good that there was a creek that ran through the ranch, as the men could go bathe after a hot itchy day in the hay fields.

It was a long days ride to gather the cattle off of the range at Hayden Hill, twelve miles away. The men would leave at four A.M. and ride out to gather. Some days they would not get home until midnight. Stan and Cleo would wait and listen for their Dad's return. When they could hear the horseshoes on the hard road and the dogs would start barking, then they knew he was about home. Some times they would load the old car with their grub and hay for the horses and go out and stay for two or three days to gather a bunch of cattle. Lawrence, John Poytress, Raymond Clark, Haskell Parks, Floyd Walker and Andy Knudsen would all ride for cattle in the Hayden Hill country.

Stan on King and Lawrence.

Many wild horses ran the Hayden Hill country in those days. Lawrence always marveled at some of the beautiful horses. Pinto's, blacks, bays and sorrels. It was quite a sight to see the stallions fighting and claiming their band of mares. The wild horses were some that were left by ranchers in the past. A lot of ranchers ranged their horses on the BLM ground and the price of horses got so cheap that they were not thorough in gathering their horses and a few were left to roam wild. They became harder and more elusive to gather. They multiplied and the Hayden Hill was over run with the wild mustangs.

When the cowboys would gather a bunch of cattle and get them separated as to what ranch they belonged to, then Lawrence would drive his on home. It was then Cleo, Stan and Avis's job to help their dad drive them on down to their Grandpa's place to feed on the bunched hay until it snowed. The cattle were then brought back to the home ranch to be fed for the winter. The steers stayed down at Kasper's and fed until they were two years old. When they were sold, they were weighed at the C.W. Clark ranch next door. Cleo can remember one year in the early 30's that her dad sold two year old steers for three cents a pound.

In 1931 it was a terrible drought and Lawrence had no hay to put up. The cattle came off of the range in July. It was such a dry year even the Rye would not grow. He had bought hay at the Fitzhugh Ranch near Canby. The cattle had to be driven the twenty five miles to the hay. The first night they made it to the far end of Round Valley and stayed at the Harrigan place. The next day they drove the cattle on over the hill to Canby. Lawrence had an old Nash car that he had cut the back out of to make a pickup. They loaded their belongings in the old car and put the milk cow in the back end. The old cow would sway from side to side and kept the car rocking. They couldn't make very good time. Finally the cow laid down then they could travel right along without her rocking the car.

One time a big draft horse, Prince, fell in an old hand dug well near the site of the original log cabin. The only way to get him out was to bring the derrick from the hay stack and sit it up at the site of the well. Even though the derrick was on skids it took most of the day to move it and set it up and securing it with stakes, cables and steel pins. It took a four horse hitch to pull old Prince out of the well. Lawrence promptly filled the old well in with the Fresno scraper.

In December of 1939 there was such a flood that the water went across the highway. It took four to six horses to pull the feed wagons. It was so muddy that the horses would mire down at the stack yard waiting for the wagon to be loaded.

The coldest winter that John Poytress can remember was the year of 1948 and 1949. The thermometer dipped to forty degrees below zero, and at noon on the sunny side of the house it might get up to zero. It was so cold that the cows mouths were frozen shut and they would follow the feed wagon in circles trying to get a bite of hay. John said that one day the team of horses were just staggering. Their noses were filled with icicles and they couldn't breath. Lawrence always said, no matter what the weather, load up your wagon as tomorrow might be worse.

Lawrence always milked a lot of cows and they sold cream to the Mountain Lily dairy at Alturas. They always had about five nurse cows in the barn and at least fifteen calves on the cows. Stan and Cleo thought it was their job to break all the calves to ride. They took their job seriously, and never left one with out breaking it to ride.

Avis, Cleo, Stan and Dale all went to the Center District school. The three older children went all eight grades there then went on to high school at Adin. Center school closed before Dale finished his eighth grade and he had to go to Bieber to school.

Kasper and Etta retired and moved to Alturas and sold their ranch to their granddaughter Avis and her husband Lee Crews.

Four generations of Weigands. Kasper, Lawrence, Stan and Doug.

Lawrence and Norma Weigand, 1956.

Lawrence Weigand.

Lawrence, Pearl, Kasper and Clara, 1961.

In 1952 Lawrence bought a neighboring ranch of 480 acres to add to his own 480 acres. Part of this ranch had been homesteaded in 1875 by C.W. Smith. Former owners had been L.D. Johnson, Ferd Chase, Leon Johnson and Ralph Holmes. John Ogburn was the owner that Lawrence bought the ranch from.

Stan moved on to the Ogburn Ranch in 1956 when he and Glorianne Roufs were married. In 1963 they moved to their own ranch and when Lawrence retired he rented it to Delmer and Leanna Hawkins a few years. Stan leased the ranch a few years, then in 1971 Cleo and her husband Harry Hunt moved back and bought the ranch from Lawrence and Norma.

Lawrence and Harry both passed away in 1981. Cleo ran the WK Ranch for several years herself. Her son David and his wife Linda and their family moved back to the ranch to make their home and work on the ranch. Norma makes her home with Cleo and still delights in talking about the old times and remembering the way it used to be.

Glorianne Weigand
February 16, 1995

The Haynes family. Back: Dick, Clara, Bessie, Fred, Etta. Front: Annie, Eva, Alvin, Birdie.

Just a Rancher's Daughter

April 28, 1995, Eva Haynes Giessner will celebrate her 101st birthday. Sharp as a tack and bright as a diamond, this daughter of a rancher still remembers remarkably well and with extreme accuracy, stories from her childhood. Her eyesight may be failing, but her love for life and her family are overwhelming.

Eva, the fifth child to be born to Richard and Clara Knoch Haynes was born in Goose Valley at the head of Goose Creek in Shasta County in North Eastern California April 8, 1894. Eleven other children were born to the young pioneering couple, making an even dozen. Those siblings were Rose, 1894, Etta 1888, Fred 1890, Alvin, 1892, Eva, 1894, Johanna, 1896, Birdie, 1898, Bessie, 1900, Sidney, 1904, Gladys, 1907, Alice, 1909, and Leland, 1912. Eva and two sisters, Birdie Bidwell, and Bessie Bosworth are the only ones still living.

Eva's father Richard W. Haynes, (Dick) was born in Buffalo Missouri in 1851. Their home was thirty five miles from Springfield, Missouri where in 1861 the Civil War was raging. Ten year old Dick could hear the cannons booming. He was scared, his father Elisha was fighting in the Union Army, while arrayed against him was Peter, Elisha's oldest son, carrying a musket in the Rebel Army.

The Haynes homestead was the dividing line between the north and the south. The family experienced the bitterness of the slavery. Murderous outlaws ranged their homeland. Brothers fighting brothers, fathers fighting sons. It was safer to be in the army than stay at home.

Dick had a sister and brother in law living in California. Wages in Missouri were sixteen dollars a month. In 1869 Dick's brother in law had told him of the gold strike in California. The gold was just laying in the stream beds waiting to be picked up. Dick had a horse he had just broken and sold him for seventy five dollars and bought a train ticket to Redding, California. That was the end of the railroad line. In October 1869 eighteen year old Dick Haynes arrived in Redding. This was only a small village with five buildings. The county seat was five miles to the West at Old Shasta.

Dick found his sister at Oak Run where she and her husband had filed for a homestead. Dick found a job building roads. This was done with a pick and shovel. Back breaking work to say the least, so he tried a little gold panning. He did not like the solitary life of a gold miner so gave that up.

In 1873 Dick headed to the famous Comstock Lode in Carson Valley, Nevada where he heard big wages were paid.

The Modoc Indian war was then being fought at the Lava Beds south of Tule Lake. As Haynes and his friend passed through Big Valley where Bieber in now located they met a band of Indians strung out nearly a mile long. They were decked in war paint and carrying bows and arrows and a few old muskets in route to help the Modocs fight their war.

After a time gold mining in Nevada, Dick decided to go back to California. He started working on the road crew again building roads for fifty cents a day. He was working for Murcken and Knoch. The terrain was steep building the road over Hatchet Mountain. The men had to be let down on ropes to pick and shovel a trail out of the mountain.

While on this job he met his future wife, Johanna Clara Knoch, the oldest daughter of Johann Fred Knoch. She was helping her mother cook for the road crew. Dick was twenty-three and he decided if he had to work so hard why not work for himself. Dick filed for a homestead on Hat Creek and he and Clara were married December 1884.

Clara's parents gave her a string of milk cows for her dowry. Dick and Clara's first two children were born in the cabin near the Carbon ranch, Rosa Leona and Etta Belle. Rosa lived only a few months. Dick traded his homestead on Hat Creek to Dick Murchen for a place on Goose Creek. He moved his family to Goose Valley at the head of the Creek to a two room log cabin with dirt floors. Dick had plans to build a sawmill and use the water power from Goose Creek to run it. He was busy draining the swamps and planting grass. His father in law Fred Knoch and brother in law Dee Knoch went to Plumas County with two wagons pulled by four horses each and brought a used sawmill back to Goose Creek.

Dick was busy putting a ranch together and building a corduroy road out of logs across the swamp so they could cross it. In 1889 Dick's brother, Cyrus and his wife with two small daughters, Cuba and Pearl came from Missouri. They lived the winter in the small log cabin with Dick and his family.

In 1892 Dick Haynes had Herman Lonquist built a large two story home for his family in Goose Valley.

Fred and Helen Knoch, Eva's grandparents. Girls: Clara, Mary and Lillie.

Clara was a hard working woman. She milked thirty cows, churned the cream to butter and pack to later be sent to market. She raised chickens and pigs and a large garden. The older children helped. Clara had a new baby every two years. Eva can remember her father calling down from the upstairs to her. He told her she had a new brother, go to the sewing machine and make him some new clothes. Eva made blankets, diapers and shirts out of flannel for the newest member of the family.

Many men in Goose Valley worked in the sawmill and cut the timber and snaked them in to the mill. When there was snow on the ground they built a "V" like contraption to snake the logs to the mill. Everyone took lumber in trade for their work. All the men needed lumber to build their homes and barns. No one had much money so they traded for what they needed. Good clear lumber sold for $10.00 a thousand. Neighbors helped neighbors and all got along very well. A lot of Indian families lived in Goose Valley and had farms with wood or log homes and barns. They worked at the Haynes mill for their lumber. Some of the Indians took the names of ranchers that they admired. The Hunt family of Indians took the name from Dan Hunt a cattleman from the valley. One family of Indians took the last name of Grant from the President of the United States, Ulysses S. Grant. The Haynes family were good friends with all of the Indians.

The Haynes children walked five miles to attend school at the Bunker Hill school house. School was held in the summer time from April to November because of the severe winters in the area. At times the older boys would miss school during haying season because they were needed on the ranch to help put up the crop.

One late fall evening, Eva, Birdie and Annie were walking the five miles home from school. Alvin had to stay to finish his examination and had sent the little girls on ahead. The children often encountered bear tracks and panther tracks on the trail to school. Their father had told them, not to turn their back on the panther, stand and face it. The little girls heard the screams of the panther, and Eva, being the oldest wondered how she could face the panther and still get down the trail home. Birdie and Annie walked down the path and Eva held on to their skirts and walked backwards all the way so she could face the panther if it approached them. They were so scared, Birdie and Annie were crying, but remembering what their father told them they kept on going. Along the path they met an Indian friend Samson Grant, who worked for their father. He said he would stay and face the panther and wait for Alvin. He told Eva to tell her father he would not be at work the next day as he was going to get that Panther. Eva can still remember the big yellow panther laying on the ground when Samson brought it in. It measured ten feet from the tip of its tail to the tip of its nose.

When Clara did the family wash the clothes line was an advertising bill board for the Fall River Milling Company. All of the underclothes were made of flour sack from the mill with their name stamped across them.

The Goose Valley Land Company, formed by two San Francisco businessmen, Wallace and Dilman intended on owning all of Goose

Valley and wanted to buy out all the homesteaders there. Many of the places were bought just for the water rights. Dick Haynes owned most of the water. If Haynes were to move he must have a suitable place to take his family.

It was 1907 and Eva was thirteen years old when they left their home at the head of Goose Creek and moved nearer to Burney. They were sad to leave the only home they had known. The children called their home Echo Dell, as you could hear the echoes from the mountains when they yelled.

Dick Haynes bought the Littrell ranch at the foot of Hatchet Mountain. It was a 1,000 acres of good meadow with lots of water and two good homes on it and a large barn. The price was $10.00 per acre. Later another two hundred acres was added to the ranch.

The children only now had three and a half miles to go to school to Burney. They drove a horse and buggy and didn't have to walk. Burney was a rough town with only three homes. There were some saloons and business's springing up. The Haynes kids were called hicks from the sticks because there were so many of them. Eva had long red curls and one of the mean boys would slap her about the head and yell fire, fire. There were teenage boys in the third grade.

Mr. Haynes was afraid his children would get into trouble with the rough necks at the new school. The Haynes children were soon sent to other school districts to go to school. It was quite common for children to be sent to other districts. There had to be at least six children at each school for them to keep a teacher. The Haynes children were sent in several different directions to live with different families. They would help with the work where they lived to help pay their way. Eva moved to Montgomery Creek to live with her teacher Agusta Marsh after she married DeForest Hobson. Eva later went to stay with her Uncle Dee Knoch and his wife Annie. She finished school at the Beaver Creek school.

When Eva finished school she went back to live with her family on the Haynes ranch and help out there. She helped with the milking and raising the huge garden.

When the Littrall family owned the ranch it had been a stopping place for travelers as it was on the main road. It was also a stop over for the stage coaches. A meal, or a bed, or feed for your horse was only twenty-five cents. The ranch was still a very busy place with the large Haynes family and a host of travelers. The huge barn had room to tie thirty two horses and at times there were teams stabled in the corrals.

In 1913 Dick bought his first automobile, a Liberty Six. Because of an injury he was never able to drive it, but his family enjoyed it.

At a family gathering when Eva was nineteen years old she met Otto Maximillian Giessner. After a courtship he asked her parents if he could marry her. They borrowed a spring wagon from DeForest Hobson who lived on Rising River, and made the two day trip to Redding to be married. The first night they stayed at the Ingot Hotel at the thriving little mining town of Ingot. The next day they went on to Redding and happened to meet up with Otto's father A.W. Giessner, Harv Wilcox and Frank Whitaker who were in Redding on a water battle. The three men from Hat Creek attended the wedding and teased the young couple unmercifully. Otto was 24 years old and Eva was 19 years old and they were married by a Judge at the Temple Hotel May 6, 1913. The young couple bought a dresser to load into their wagon and started the two day journey home. Their first night they stayed at the Spears stage stop at Montgomery Creek. Eva calls this two story yellow home that still stands along side of the highway her honeymoon cottage.

Otto Giessner took his new bride to Hat Creek to his cabin. He had taken up a pre-emption and had started his cattle ranch there. Otto and his brother Herman had been pretty much on their own since they were young boys. Their mother had fallen off of a barn when she was eight months pregnant. She had been helping with the roofing of the barn when she slipped and fell. The baby was born, but died, and Otto's mother also died.

Otto and Eva raised beef cattle and had several milk cows. Eva made butter to sell to the neighbors. They delivered milk to the Pit 1 power plant. Soon a creamery was started at Cassell and the farmers on Hat Creek had a place to sell their milk and cream. When P.G.&E. came in to the country the farmers could sell all of the milk, eggs and meat that they wanted. There was a big demand for even garden produce to feed the crews building the power plants and lines.

When Otto first brought Eva to Hat Creek they moved into a small cabin. The boards on the walls ran up and down and the wind blew right through it. In 1926 they moved the cabin over and built a new home in its place. Eva still lives in that home.

Otto loved his horses and livestock. They used many teams of horses to do the haying and farming. They was quite a demand for good draft horses. Otto and some friends from Big Valley, the Kramers and Gerigs went into partners and bought a beautiful Percheron Stallion to breed their mares. The stallion, named Frank was used for their own mares and was used to breed many of the neighbors mares. Otto broke teams to sell to other ranchers.

Eva and Otto had five sons. August Richard born 1913, Elmer Otto born 1915, Rudolph Elbert born 1918, Emil Fredick born 1920 and died

Wedding picture of Otto and Eva Giessner, 1913.

Otto Giessner with Percheron Stallion "Frank", owned by Giessners,
Kramers and Gerigs. 1913.

L. to R.: Dick and Clara Haynes, 50th wedding anniversary, Clara's father Fred Knoch,
sister Mary Murer and brother Dee Knoch, 1934.

Eva and Otto Giessner.

at seven months, and Lawrence Alten born 1923 and died of scarlet fever at five years.

May 1915 the phone rang and it was a warning that Mt. Lassen was erupting. All of the neighbors were fleeing their homes and getting to higher ground as there was a terrible flood coming. Eva did not know what to pack. They loaded their trunks into their wagon and took blankets

Eva Giessner, 100th birthday.

to wrap the children in and some food and headed to a high knoll and spent the night under a big pine tree. The flood came, but they were so far down the creek that all they got was a lot of muddy water.

Although Eva and Otto had no girls they had many girls stay with them as well as several other boys that needed a home. Eva's sister Birdie Bidwell lived farther down on Hat Creek and the school bus did not go that far, so Birdie's daughters, Maxine, Marjorie and Virginia all stayed with Eva so they could go to high school in McArthur.

Eva's parents Dick and Clara Haynes celebrated their 50th wedding anniversary in 1934. Clara wore her wedding dress that she had been married in. Her father Fred Knoch was there to give his daughter away a second time to the same man. Dick and Clara still lived on the Haynes ranch and their sons, Alvin, Sidney and Leland ran the ranch. Clara died in 1954 at the age of 85 and Dick died in 1974 at the age of 95.

Eva's and Otto's three sons were not the lover of horses that their father was, but they loved to run the big machinery.

While in high school August Haynes surveyed the first ball diamond in McArthur. Elmer surveyed the road from Hat Creek to Cayton Valley. August put in the first pipe line for P.G.& E. He surveyed the gas line from Alaska to the San Francisco bay area. Rudolph was the mechanic in the family. Eva said if it was broke Rudolph could fix it. Eva is very proud of her son's accomplishments. Whether it be logging, surveying or running large equipment building roads, Eva said her sons could do it.

August married Helen Miller and they had two children. Elmer married Jewel Owen and they had two children.

Otto passed away in 1956, and August and Elmer have both passed away.

Rudolph married Checkers Parry and they have five children. Rudolph now runs the Giessner ranch and Checkers stays with Eva in her home where Eva is most comfortable. Eva has nine grandchildren, fifteen great grandchildren and thirteen great great grandchildren.

Eva has enjoyed many Grange tours with her sister Bessie. They have been across the USA four times. To Alaska, Australia, New Zealand and Hawaii. She has traveled from horse and buggy to the Jet age and in helicopters and dune buggies. A charter member of the Inter-Mountain Cattlewomen, she was Cowbelle Mom of the year in 1972. Honorary Life Member of the PTA. A member of the Eastern Star and they had a Home Economics club that made pajamas for the soldiers during WWI. August was in the Navy and Elmer was in the Army during WWI, so it made Eva feel good to be making things for the soldiers.

When asked what her formula for her long healthy life was, she commented "I didn't smoke nor drink hard liquor. Went to bed early, got up early, loved to work and eat lots of BEEF." Eva has always kept busy and happy. It is a good life and still is. She had a whopping big 100th birthday party and is planning her 101st.

Eva said, "I'm just a rancher's daughter that married a rancher. I just remember the advice my father gave to us children when the panther stalked us. Don't turn your back, just go ahead and face your problems, stay with it and you'll get it done."

Glorianne Weigand
March 18, 1995

The Leventon family.
Back row:
Itha, Joyce.
Front row:
Hilda, Joe,
Nettie and Donald.

The Blacksmith of Lookout

In the late 1800's every town had a blacksmith shop and the local blacksmith. He was an important man in the town and was needed to shoe the horses, repair the wagon wheels, sharpen the plow shares and build the wagons. Lookout, California in the corner of Modoc County in northeastern California was no exception. The sign on the blacksmith shop that still stands today reads 1888, J.W. LEVENTON, BLACK-SMITH. The blacksmith shop stands deserted in the middle of the little hamlet of Lookout. The hitching rail out front is a reminder of the many horses that were at one time tied there waiting to be shod or of buggy horses tied there to have a little repair work done or someone that just stopped by for a visit. It was a lively place and at one time five men were employed by Joe Leventon to keep up with the work that was demanded by the local farmers and ranchers. They built several wagons and in 1918 they built a covered wagon for a sheep man from Merrill, Oregon, Mr. O'Conner. He needed the wagon to tend his sheep that ranged a large portion of northern California and southern Oregon. The Blacksmith shop closed in 1936 as times were changing and there was not much of a need for the works of a blacksmith.

The small building next to the famous blacksmith shop has a history of its own. This cabin was said to be older than Lookout itself. The little building was built in 1870 and sit across the river. It was a saloon at one time and in 1874 it was the post office after it was moved to its present location.

Lookout was originally known as Riverside. The area of Riverside was founded in 1860. In 1868 Bob Whitley was the first man to settle in Lookout. He built a cabin and trading post. In 1870 the Moses Carmichael family came to the area and started a sawmill. 1873 John Marcus was listed as the Justice of the Peace and the Deputy Sheriff.

In 1875 the business section of Lookout included Stephen Mooers from Maine, dealer in general merchandise; E. Breeder, Carriage and wagon maker; O.T. Smith, manufacturer of harness and saddlery; M.

Calkins from New York, dairyman and cheese maker; John Marcus from Missouri, carpenter; Gordon and Johnson, manufacturers of spokes and shingles;, Morton Sonberger from Vermont, Photographer; A. Tebbs, blacksmith and wagon-maker; Henry Loncor from Illinois, Postmaster; and James Whitley from Ohio, keeper of the hotel and livery stable. In 1877 Captain Mooers closed his store and moved to Adin, a town eleven miles east. After a time Riverside started to decline. Under the continuing arrival of settlers, it soon made a substantial recovery. In 1880 the Brownell Brothers of Bieber opened a store.

In 1880 the post office was re-established and Riverside was renamed Lookout.

"LOOKOUT! We have surrendered 'Riverside' without recrimination", a resident wrote in a local paper. While the latter may be known as out dwelling place, the former is known as a healthy thriving little village.

The name of Lookout was believed to derive its name from a nearby hill where it is said the Pit River Indians kept a lookout to warn against raids by the Modoc Indians. Lookout is also the site of the last lynching in 1901 when five men were hung. This event stopped the cattle rustling and horse thievery in this part of the old west. There were some who said at the time that this represented a return to the good old days of the Gold Rush when crimes were dealt with surely and swiftly.

Joe Leventon came to the town of Lookout in 1880. He was born in Fiddletown, Amador County, California in 1860. Joe had two sisters in the area and that is the reason he came to this little town on the Pit River. One sister Sarah, and her husband, Eli Trowbridge ran the store in Lookout. Another sister Kate was married to L.C. Morris.

When Joseph Leventon came to this territory now called Lookout there was only a blacksmith shop, livery stable and a hotel.

The young Leventon helped build the old dance hall in 1882. The pay was six bits a day and you boarded yourself. He also carried the mail from Bieber to Timber Mountain then to Steel Swamp. He made one trip a week. Joe and his brother Robert homesteaded a timber claim, but later sold it.

Robert Leventon came to the Modoc country in 1879, a year before Joe. He worked on ranches in the area when the wages were board and room and a dollar a month and a pair of new overalls once a year.

The original Leventon ranch had been homesteaded in 1872 by James Whitley. He first homesteaded a 160 acres parcel, then later he added another 160. This gave him 320 acres that he sold to A.A. Lieuallen and his wife Sarah in 1883. Lieuallen sold the property to Robert and Joseph Leventon 1888, although the deed was not transacted until 1898, The ranch is the southern boundary of the town of Lookout, and is still in the Leventon family today, owned and operated by Joe's grandson Dean and his wife Dixie.

Joe and Robert had leased the property for quite some time before the purchase. They had written to the owners, Lieuallen and Whitley and offered them $2,500.00 for the ranch. In the meantime Lieuallen and Whitley had a letter in route to the Leventons asking them a lower price for the ranch. The letters crossed in the mail and Leventons had to pay the higher price for the ranch.

Joe and Robert Leventon raised horses and mules and matched teams to sell. Some of the teams were broke to work and some were not.

An advertisement in Modoc County in 1912 read; LEVENTON BROS. LOOKOUT, CAL., LOOKOUT FEED & LIVERY STABLE; LOOKOUT BLACKSMITH SHOP; BREEDERS OF THOROUGH-BRED GERMAN COACH AND BLACK PERCHERON HORSES, DURHAM CATTLE, AND BERKSHIRE SWINE. DEALERS IN LIVESTOCK.

Joe Leventon married Nettie Crowley in 1896. The Crowley family had run the hotel at Chalk Ford, now known as Bieber. They later moved near Egg Lake, eight miles from Lookout and homesteaded there.

Joe had bought a place from Mr. Laird. There was a home on the property, and Joe wanted to move the house to his property a half mile

Leventon hay crew, 1909.

away in the town of Lookout. They jacked the house up and put it on four wagons and pulled the wagons with teams and moved the house to its present location.

When Joe took Nettie as his bride he moved her to the home he had moved and they raised their children there. One son Daryl died when he was a few months old. The other four children Joyce, Itha, Hilda and Don were all born in this house.

Itha married Clinton Fulcher, Joyce married Floyd Walker then later Joseph Weldon, Donald married Gwendolyn Auble and Hilda married Carrol Morrison.

In 1918 Joe and Nettie moved in to the house next door and Donald moved into their home.

Nettie Leventon was a Mid-Wife and helped deliver over three hundred babies in Big Valley. She worked for Dr. Tinsman at Adin, she helped nurse many people of the valley back to health.

In an interview for the California Grange news in 1949 of Nettie Leventon, she said she was born in Mendocino County, California March 30, 1869. Her family moved to Big Valley in Modoc County in 1881. she had four brothers and three sisters. Families were unable to travel very far so the family ties were much closer and stronger than they are today. The had to travel on horseback or by wagon or cart, so there were few pleasure trips.

They did have a few neighborhood parties and dances in the homes. The only dances were square dances, Scottishes and polkas.

Nettie's mother helped the sick and that is how she got into nursing and being a mid-wife. She felt it was her duty to help the sick whenever possible. And she enjoyed the work a lot. She felt babies was her most important job and she help deliver so many babies she had lost count, but did know that she had delivered one generation and when they grew up she delivered the second generation of the same family.

Nettie was an energetic worker and a tireless woman. She not only raised her own family, but ran a boarding house. Wendell Durkee was one of the boarders that stayed the summer while he was cruising timber for the Red River Lumber Company. Wentzell Broadzeller the owner of the local creamery also boarded with the family.

When the first telephones were installed in the Lookout area the switchboard was put into the Leventon home and Nettie was the switchboard operator.

Robert Leventon and his family moved to Modesto, California in 1911. He sold his part of the ranch to his brother Joe in 1910. Later the family moved to Manteca where Robert owned a blacksmith shop.

Back row: Gwen, Donald. Front row L. to R.: Jerry, Dean, Janice and Gabe.

In 1914 a church was built in Lookout and Joe Leventon was one of the trustees. He had donated part of his ranch property for the church. The school and the park were also built on part of the Leventon ranch property.

In 1937 Joe turned over a half interest in the ranch to his son Donald, and in 1939, he turned over the complete interest. Joe passed away in

1940. Nettie had a stroke which left her disabled for twelve years. She passed away in 1958.

"Papa" as Joe was called by his grandchildren always smoked a corn cob pipe. Most of the time it was upside down and unlit, but always a part of him. He enjoyed nailing a board on a fence or doing small odd jobs on the ranch for many years.

Donald had married Gwendolen Auble of Adin. Her grandfather, Irvin Shepard had the flour mill along Ash Creek in that town. It was powered by a water wheel. Many of the valley farmers took their grain to that mill to be ground into flour. Donald and Gwen had four children, Donald Junior (Gabe), Jerry, Janice and Dean.

When Donald had gone to school the school house was across the river. They later built one in the main part of town. All of the Leventon children went to Lookout to school for the first eight years, then went to Adin to high school.

Gabe married Betty Holcomb and they had four children.

Jerry married Lorraine Carrol and they had one son.

Janice married W.O. (Jim) Holcomb and they had four children.

Dean married Dixie Ash and they had two children.

The Pit River flooded in the 1930's, but never got into town. All of the surrounding fields were flooded. The cattle business was pretty depressed in those years. A cow buyer would look at the cattle and offer you two cents and head for the gate. You had no argument and had to

The case tractor and first baler on the Leventon ranch.

take his price or not sell. In 1934 Donald had steers on the Vogt place on pasture near Adin. He drove them twelve miles to the stockyards at the railroad at West Bieber and was paid three cents a pound and they were weighed there after the long drive.

The driest year that Donald had remembered was 1924. They put up sixty tons of hay on the whole ranch where now they put up 700 ton. The Pit River went dry. That fall they drove cattle to the Cyril Schott ranch south of Bieber to feed them hay. Donald stayed there to feed them. When that hay was gone they drove them many miles to the west to Egg Lake and fed them hay they had bought from Louis Kramer. That hay had been in the barn for twelve years and was hard as a rock. That year it was just dry and cold and no rain or snow

July 5, 1933 a devastating fire ravaged the small town of Lookout. The fire started in Leventons barn and was thought to be spontaneous

Donald and Gwen Leventon, 1941.

combustion. Jerry was eight years old and he and Gabe were just ready to go gather the milk cows to bring them in for their evening milking. A man sitting on the porch of the store across the street yelled fire as the whole barn just blew up. There was a strong wind blowing and the fire quickly moved down the street, burning everything in its path. It burned the south side of the street, then jumped the road and burned homes and barns on the north side. It finally burned itself out. The closest fire truck was at Bieber, six miles away and even when it got there, nothing could be done. Eleven buildings were consumed before the fire was contained. Fulcher's Ford garage, the Ice Cream Parlor and Pool Hall, Kenny's Hotel, the home and garage of D. Moss, the home and barn of Hitchcocks, the store and home of Z. Cheney, Leventons milk barn, granary and horse barn. All of Leventons harness, saddles and hay equipment burned except for what the two teams in the field had on their backs.

Leventons had to replace the milk barn as soon as possible as they were milking 25-30 cows in the open corrals. They installed a milking machine in the new barn. Cheney rebuilt a small store and Fulcher rebuilt his garage.

In 1953 Leventons rebuilt their granary.

Another devastating fire in Lookout destroyed the big general store in 1963. Charlie Bietel had owned the store for many years and just six months before had sold it to a Mr. Horton.

The Leventon family did as many families of that time did, they milked many cows. Donald thought it was a starvation job, but the cream check was sometimes the only income the family had for ready cash. They raised many hogs, farrowing out about thirty sows. The skimmed milk was mixed with the grain the family raised to fatten out their many feeder pigs. When it was time to market the hogs in the early days, they were driven to market. Some were taken as far as Merrill, Oregon. They would take a horse drawn cart and a grain wagon and head up through the timber. The first few days were the hardest, but soon the pigs learned to follow the grain wagon and the going was much easier. They also drove hogs to Madeline nearly fifty miles to the railroad.

In later years most of their hogs were sold to Crum Meat Company and at the local auction yard. Now with the meat market no longer in business and a decline in grain production the hogs are no longer part of the Leventon operation.

Donald was a perfectionists when it came to stacking hay. He liked nice large neat stacks. Homer Robinson and Nolan Fulcher were some of the mainstays during haying season. Gabe and Jerry were old enough to drive derrick and clean up around the stack.

Gabe and Jerry both went into the Army and Dean went into the Air Force. When the boys left home it was time for Donald to buy his first baler. In 1943 they ordered the case baler from Tulelake, California, and the dealer was slow in getting it delivered. It was a case poke and tie baler and it took three men to operate it and another to drive the baler. The hay was getting dry and Donald was anxious to get started. They had to cross a bridge across the slough of Pit River and as they did so, the bridge broke and the baler fell through. It took three days to jack it up and get it off of the bridge. Donald was working on the baler and Mike Carmichael and Martin Courtright were helping him. When the hay would hang up it would throw the belt and stop the baler. This particular time the belt was not thrown and as Donald kicked the hay loose the plunger started and nearly crushed Donald. Martin pulled him free just in time.

The baler was taken to Sam Gerigs and Homer Jacks to do custom haying for them.

The many acres of grain the Leventons grew was harvested by stationary harvesters or contract harvesters. Albert Joiner was one of the men with a harvester.

A cook wagon was drawn by a team of horses from field to field where the men were working. A cook was hired to cook for the men.

The irrigating for the ranch was done from the water from Pit River. In early years it was done by flooding, but now is done with pumps and wheel lines.

A slaughter house was on the ranch. Hogs were butchered once a year late in the fall when the meat could be kept during the cooler weather. Several dozen hogs would be butchered at a time and the hams and bacons would be cured and smoked.

The fat was cut into large pieces an put into a large kettle outside with a fire built underneath it. The fat had to be stirred all the time it was being melted down into lard. The lard was run through a lard press and strained an poured into large containers. The sausage was ground and seasoned and cooked into patties. They were stored in large crocks and the lard was poured over them to keep them for the families use.

In the winter when the Pit river froze over, the locals used ice saws to cut blocks of ice from the river. It was stored in blocks in the community ice house. The ice kept for many months. Everyone helped in harvesting the ice and everyone shared the ice as they needed it.

In the late 1950's Donald bought a ranch from Roy Courtright that enlarged the present Leventon ranch to over 400 acres. Donald also bought Kate Gerig's cows to increase his cow herd.

Donald and Gwen have left their children to carry on the legends and traditions of the Leventon family.

Gabe worked on the home ranch when he was younger before he went into the Army. He drove logging trucks and worked in the local mills.

Jerry worked on the ranch, then went into the Army, he later ran the Potter ranch for ten years. After that he worked for the Modoc County road department for 26 years.

Janice helped her mother with the cooking for the family and hay crews before she married.

Dean went to college a couple years, then into the Air Force then back to work on the ranch.

All of Donald and Gwen's children had a share in the growth and operation of the Leventon ranch.

Cattle and hay are now the main crops raised on the ranch. Dean has some Forest Service permit, but most of the summer his cattle range on private pasture that he rents.

In 1988 Donald sold the Leventon ranch to his son Dean. This was 100 years from the time the first sign was put on the Leventon Blacksmith Shop in 1888. And they are still going strong.

Glorianne Weigand
April 20, 1995

From Wagon Trains to Cattlemen

"A GOLD STRIKE AT HAYDEN HILL" *Adin Argus*, July 26, 1883.

On Wednesday, July 30, 1883 another rich strike was made in the Juniper mine, Hayden Hill, Lassen County. The new strike which has disclosed a mine almost as rich as Alladin's famous discovery is on the 90 foot level, and is also tapped at the 60 foot level. The vein is fifteen inches wide and is known to extend for a considerable distance. Although in the past the Juniper mine has made many thousands of dollars for its owners, nothing more rich and expensive than this strike has ever been found. A large amount of the dirt it is reported yields $5.00 to the pound.

As an illustration of the richness of the ore it is stated that one man is getting $2,000.00 per day. Very rich dirt has been found in this mine heretofore, but what makes the present strike so valuable is the extent as well as the richness of the lead. If we should state that a sheet of gold, an inch in thickness, extending several rods in every direction had been discovered in the Juniper the non professional would appreciate the value of this new strike, and yet such a statement would hardly be an exaggeration.

Juniper mine has heretofore been valued at $600,000.00 but that amount of money would not approach buying it today. The owners of the new Golconda; are John McFarling (discover and original locator), heirs of J.W. Harvey, Rosebery Knight and Harvey and John Cyrus of Calistoga.

But Juniper is not alone in her good fortune. Harbert Brothers in running a cross cut from their main shaft, 125 feet below the surface have struck an extensive body of ore which brings $25.00 to $45.00 per ton. In putting their quartz mill in order, preparations for making a run and their many old friends will be satisfied to learn that their prospects are very bright.

The Golden Eagle Mine, Hopkins and Nash and Company proprietors has also struck a ledge three feet wide with defined walls and the company has every reason to expect rich results. The Golden Eagle has been

Hayden Hill, Easter Sunday 1888.

pronounced by competent judges to be the best mine on Hayden Hill. It is well developed and many large beds of paying ore are exposed.

Among other miners whose names we have mentioned in connection with the present BOOM at Hayden Hill are Richie and Dunbar, who are working Hoes' Brothers Brush Hill claim. They have taken out from 50 to 60 tons of fine ore and are milling the same. Lacert and Company are also prospering in the Hayden Gouge.

In a local paper from Big Valley on July 31, 1890 the following story appeared. TWO MEN SMOTHER TO DEATH IN A BURNING MINE—NARROW ESCAPE FOR OTHERS.

One of the saddest occurrences that has ever taken place in this section of the country happened last Thursday afternoon at Hayden Hill, whereby two men, Frank Auble and W.A. Dunbar lost their lives and several others came near being suffocated in trying to rescue them.

Between three and four o'clock the shaft house of the Eclipse Mine was discovered to be on fire, and Messrs Auble and Dunbar were known to be at work down in the mine. The shaft house was built directly over the shaft, and adjoining it was the blacksmith shop. When the fire was first seen the building was falling in.

Mr. Auble was known to have been at work at the forge in the afternoon and it is supposed that the fire originated from the coals that were left in the forge, as a heavy wind was blowing at the time.

The shaft is 80 feet deep with a drift running to 40 feet from the surface and another at the bottom, the two drifts being connected by a raise or slope. The two men were working in a winze off from the 80 foot drift. Of course when the timbers from the burning building began to fall, some of them fell into the shaft.

From all indications, the two men, when they discovered the fire, seeing no chance to escape by the shaft from the 80 foot level went up to the 40 foot level through the slope, thinking, perhaps they might escape up the shaft from that level. All the candles were on the 80 foot level, and when the bodies were discovered on the 40 foot level, the candles were near them, which was evidence that they had time to go below again and get the candles.

After the fire was put out by the miners and mill men, who had been apprised of the terrible danger in which their two comrades were situated, Ed Highett was sent down, but could not descend but a little way on account of the foul air. When he was brought to the surface he was so badly suffocated that it took ten to fifteen minutes to bring him to. The air was so foul that a candle would not burn ten feet from the surface.

Next a rope was placed around W.C. Howard, which precaution was taken whenever a man went down, who was lowered to the bottom of the shaft but had to be raised again immediately.

A message was then sent to Adin to send up all the hose in town, which was promptly done, (Adin being some fifteen miles or more away.) Ed Haley and Wm. Chisolm taking it up, arriving at the mine about 3 o'clock A.M. The hose was attached to a billows and run down in the mine, through which air was pumped until 10 o'clock a.m. when it was considered that a man could go down without danger of suffocation.

Montgomery Auble brother of one of the unfortunate men, went down to the 40 foot level and entered to the end, where he found both bodies, Frank Auble laying with his head against the end of the drift, face downward, and Mr. Dunbar with his head at Mr. Auble's feet, was lying in the same position. Both men had their hats tightly clinched in their hands, as if the last act of their lives was to fan themselves to get good air.

The article tells of the rescue of the bodies and the near asphyxiation of the rescuers and trying to revive them. Nearly twenty-four hours passed from the time of the fire to the time the bodies were rescued. Mr. Auble left two children, his wife having died eight years before. Mr. Dunbar who was only 36 years old left his wife and three small children.

William Dunbar known as Billy was the son of a Merchant Master out of Brewster Barnstable, Mass. who had his own sailing ship. He sailed cargo between Astoria, Oregon and the Orient.

On December 29, 1879 Billy Dunbar married Sarah Waite in Adin, Calif. Seven children were born to them in the mining town of Hayden Hill. All but three children died in infancy. Ruth, Ernest and Edith lived to adulthood.

After the tragic mine accident Sarah's father, Fredrick M. Waite and her youngest brother, Ben Waite took the family under their wing and took Sarah and the children to Adin to live with them. Edith was born in 1888 and was only two years old. Ben built a box on the plow that he pulled with his horses so she could ride with him. When she tired she would sleep in the box. Ben Waite never married he just took care of his niece and her family.

When the tragic mine accident claimed the lives of Billie Dunbar and his partner they were just getting it developed. It had the prospects of being one of the richest on the hill. The death of her husband left Sarah destitute and penniless. The Eclipse Mine was taken by the state for back taxes of $10.92 in 1890. The assessed value of the mine was $575.00. Delinquent poll taxes and penalties accrued and made the total that it was sold to the state for $22.97. By 1902 the Dunbar estate was able to reclaim their one half interest of the Eclipse mine for $105.01

Edith Dunbar's grandparents, the Waite family came into California with the train of 100 wagons led by Jefferson Hunt in 1849, the first wagon train to come into California over Cajon Pass, the western end of the Sante Fe Trail. The train organized near Springfield, Missouri. Some detoured to other trails, some stopped off along the way.

Many hardships were encountered by the slow moving train and their provisions were gone. Hunger soon stalked the immigrants and some of the oxen were killed to eat. Others died and the wagons were made into carts.

The pass was so rough they had to take the wagons apart and take one wheel at a time over the boulders and slide the axles over the trees on the trail known as the Santa Fe Trail. The pioneers narrowly escaped drowning in a flood in 1849. When the Waites first entered San Bernardino, Calif. there was only one Indian Hacienda. The famished immigrants traveled on to the Slover Ranch near Aqua Mansa. Mr. Slover opened his smokehouse and supplied them with bacon and squash of which they partook so freely without cooking, that seven to nine of the party died and were buried along the trail. They went to Los Angeles where James Waite purchased the *Los Angeles Star* newspaper which he ran for several years and in 1855 became the postmaster of that little town. Later they traveled on to a tent city, known as San Francisco.

James Waite kept moving north and bought a newspaper business. He became a very wealthy and prosperous man. His granddaughter Sarah Mariah Waite (daughter of Fredrick) who was born in 1860 married William Dunbar in 1879. William (Billie) Dunbar was the victim of the fire in the mine shaft in 1890 where he lost his life at Hayden Hill.

Sarah's brother Ben was a teamster and had freight wagons that he hauled freight to and from the Big Valley area. Ben and his father hauled the lumber for the church in Adin from Conklin's sawmill on Adin Mountain in 1888 with their team and wagon.

The children of Sarah and Billie, Edith and her sister Ruth and brother Ernest went to the Providence school.

Edith grew to be a delightful young woman. She and a friend Ivy Bath went to Susanville to take the Lassen County teaching exam. In 1907 Edith received her teaching credential and taught at schools in Secret Valley, Doyle, Providence, Lookout and Likely during her career. In 1913 she was awarded a Life Diploma in teaching.

While Edith taught at Providence, she and her mother, Sarah, lived in the Ladies Club Hall in Adin. Also living in the Club Hall was Amy Myers from Lookout, who was attending the Wilson Preparatory School in Adin. Amy invited Edith to spend the weekend with her in Lookout. While there, Edith heard a young man singing downstairs and asked Amy who that was. Amy told her it was her brother Jim. James Randolph Myers Jr. was born in 1883 at Clover Swale and was the sixth of ten children. A romance soon sparked.

Jim's father James Randolph Myers Sr. had come from Alabama in the 1830's. He owned a ranch at Clover Swale, but decided to move to Lookout and build a Hotel. He was hoping to make his fortune on the travelers going through that area.

Jim worked on ranches when he was a young man. He and a good friend Jeff Eades worked together and were good buckaroos. Jim also worked on many ranches on the threshing and haying crews.

In 1901 the Myers Hotel was the place that the Sheriff was holding the Hall gang the night they were lynched.

In 1913 James Randolph Myers Jr. married Edith Dunbar in Pittville, California and they moved to the Dixie Valley ranch. Jim was a carpenter and built a barn at Dixie Valley among many other buildings in other areas.

After moving to Fall River Mills in 1914 their first three children were born. In 1914 Norris was born, in 1915 Melvin was born, Evelyn was born in 1917.

Uncle Ben Waite with his freight wagon at Bear Flat, near Bartle, 1912.

Jim Myers and Edith Dunbar, 1913.

Clint Fulcher and Jim Myers in front of the Myers Hotel in Lookout, 1912.

Jim did carpenter work in Fall River Mills and drove the stage to Bartle. The family moved to Anderson for a short time, where Jim worked on a flume.

In 1919 Jim and Edith moved to the Adin area near Rush Creek. Jim built the bridge spanning the Pit River in Stone Coal Valley, he worked on the Adin High School Gym and the grammar school. He built the old school house in Bieber and the Lookout Grange Hall and the addition at the Providence school house.

Jim Myers had a sawmill on Rush Creek. They lived there several years. Norris and Melvin were ready to start school and their mother started them the same year as they were only thirteen months apart. She taught them at home as there was not a school nearby.

While at Rush Creek, Dolores was born in 1921 and died three days later. Because this birth left Edith with a leaky heart valve, she went to Adin to be cared for by Lizzie Blair when James Delbert was born in 1922.

After leaving the sawmill at Rush Creek Jim took his horses and went to Susanville to log. When one of his horses broke its leg Jim turned back to carpentry.

The family moved again in the spring of 1926 to Janesville where they lived while Jim built the highway maintenance station. They moved back to Susanville in 1927 for Edith to be close to a doctor for the birth of Benjamin.

The family moved back to Adin and in the summer of 1929 Jim rented what was known as the Briscoe place from Frank Studley. The Studley family had lived there for quite some time, but had moved to the 101 Ranch after Frank's father had died. The Myers family raised turkeys, grain and hogs and bought some milk cows from Earl Auble. The family was pretty self sufficient. The branding iron they used on their cattle was the circle box that was Grand Dad Myers horse brand. It is still used by Melvin Myers today.

Norris Myers had a love for mechanics and started working in the Adin Garage for Beavis Ash when he was a young man. Melvin loved the ranching business and worked for neighbors Floyd Walker and Vet Niles on their ranches.

Jim Myers continued to do carpentry work in Big Valley, his last work was done on the Traugh house in Adin. In 1932 he planted a crop of grain he would not see harvested. He became very sick on July 4 that year with what was diagnosed as appendicitis. Norris drove his parents to Susanville, where Jim had an appendectomy and where he died on July 25.

Cowboys at Lookout. Bill Gould, Hillery Myers, Clarence Myers, Elwood Leventon, Jim Myers, Joe Craig, Jeff Eades, George Farmer, Arch Eades, unknown, A. Cannon, a dude, Dorris Eades, Archie or Everett Criss.

Edith and her children, with the help of her Uncle Ben Waite, met the challenge of life without their husband and father. Edith took over a homestead near the ranch and proved up on it while taking care of her family. The young Myers boys were left with a big responsibility. Not only a ranch to run, but they helped their Mother and younger brothers and sister. Delbert was only ten and Ben was only five. They looked up to Melvin like a father.

Norris took over the garage from Beavis Ash in 1937. In 1941 the garage and several other buildings in Adin burned. The garage building was owned by Ira Nelson and he rebuilt it. Norris went on with the business until 1952. Norris had married Irma Bassett and they moved to her parents place to run it when they retired. Irma and Norris have three children, Daran, Hal, and Starla.

Melvin, Ben, Delbert and Norris Myers, June 1984.

In 1934 Melvin decided he wanted to be a rancher and he went to Mr. Studley and asked to buy the ranch. He rented it for several years and in 1944 he bought the ranch. Before that time Melvin had bought the Chace Valley ranch from Vern Iverson. Later he added the Henderson, Iverson, Dunbar, Chace and his mothers homestead to his holdings, making his present ranch quite productive with cattle and grain.

Melvin married Lovine Mayben and they have two children, Lura and Darrell.

When Delbert was old enough he worked on the Forest Service fire crew in 1942. He was on the first fire crew. He then worked for the county then went into the service. Delbert was a tank operator in Austria. When he returned to the states he worked for Norris in the garage and Melvin on the ranch. Later he bought a service station of his own.

Delbert married Keith (Tiny) Baker.

Evelyn married Omar Coppedge and they have two children, Beth and Jim.

Ben went into the service and lived his lifelong dream and was a pilot. Still flying today he trains pilots. Ben married Hazel Green and they have two children Melody and Ben.

The Myers heritage is a long and exciting one. From wagon trains, to Hotels, mining, farming and ranching. It is a life that none could claim as dull, but shows a dynamic family that had to survive and struggle to keep their ancestry what it is today.

> Glorianne Weigand
> May 17, 1995

A Cattle Baron's Dream

The Civil War was over and two brothers that were veterans of that war decided to travel to the untamed West. George and Ira Mapes turned their horses west from the state of Michigan and left their families to start a new life in the land of opportunity. Records show that they arrived in the town of Reno, Nevada in the early 1880's. George was somewhat handicapped as he had lost an arm while hunting bear. The bear wasn't at fault, but the loss of his arm was from a gun shot wound.

George and Ira had a little money between the two of them and they bought a piece of property and opened a feed store. The location of the Mapes feed store is now the location of the famous Mapes Hotel in Reno.

Reno was a small town and the feed store was not busy enough for the two brothers, so Ira left George to cater to the needs of the local people and their livestock. Ira went to Santa Rosa and started in the hotel business in that town.

George got into some fast money deals. Banks could lend money to themselves and he had shares in the bank. George started buying up cattle and was one of the "BIG FIVE", known throughout the west. The Big Five were cattle and land barons that owned and controlled thousands of acres of land and thousands of head of cattle. Members of that elite group were, George Mapes, Henry Miller, Dan Brown, Pete French and Robert McConnaughey. Henry Miller owned thousands of acres throughout the west with his partner Charles Lux. They were known as the "Cattle Kings". Pete French did not own any cattle, but was the cow boss for Dr. Glenn and trailed thousands of head of cattle from Glenn County, California through the Lassen County country into Oregon. Dan Brown was a banker and controlled large finances. McConnaughey was the owner of the famous MC ranch in south eastern Oregon.

In the winter of 1888 and 1889 George Mapes lost 5,000 head of cattle in the severe blizzards and snow from starvation. Cattle weren't worth anything anyhow so he felt he really didn't lose much. George had ranches all over Northern California, Oregon and Nevada. He owned a large ranch near Burns, Oregon that he sold to the Fish and Game for six hundred thousand dollars.

George owned half of the Sierra Valley. Ira Mapes and his family returned from Santa Rosa and worked for George at Beckworth in Sierra Valley. The ranch there consisted of 3,000 acres.

With all the turn of events the feed store in Reno was torn down and a post office was built in its place. Later the post office was moved and George's son Charlie bought the property back and built the Mapes Hotel, one of the largest and most popular hotels in Reno. Hard times hit with the depression and Charlie lost the hotel to his creditors. The Mapes Hotel is no longer in the family, but still carries the name of one of the famous big five.

Ira and his wife were working hard at Beckworth and plans for starting a herd of cattle and a ranch of their own was in progress.

Their family was growing and they had six children, James,(born in Santa Rosa in 1876) and his brother, Press and sisters Lottie, Ida, Georgia and Katherine.

A cousin, George Mapes and his wife Nettie who lived at Beckworth had five children. All five of their children died one winter of diphtheria and are all buried in the Beckworth cemetery.

Ira moved his family to Litchfield in Lassen County and started ranching there, still working for George, who had bought the ranch at a Sheriff sale for $11,000 for 1100 acres.

This ranch was originally the McKezick Cattle Company. McKezick had bought an option on all the wool in the West for $1.00 a pound. The bottom dropped out and wool went down to .30 cents a pound. McKezick was holding all the contracts and the transaction broke them. McKezick was a big operator and ran thousands of head of cattle and at one time drove two hundred and twenty five head of bulls through the Mapes ranch. Mr. McKezick was a senator from Nevada and Dunn was his cow boss. Their main ranch was at Doyle with a mansion at that headquarters ranch. McKezick made some bad business decisions and along with the wool deal he was a devastated man.

Ira's son Jim Mapes had grown up and he married Donna Short from Pittville, Calif. The Short family had moved to Standish in 1910 and Jim and Donna were married in 1911. They had three children, Madaline, Milton and Julian. Julian was born in 1915 at Litchfield.

Julian went to school at Standish being taught by his Aunt Katherine Mapes. Milton and Madaline had no inclination to live a rural life and moved to larger towns and the bright lights. This left Julian to be the rancher in the family.

When George Mapes died, Ira bought out the Litchfield ranch from the Mapes estate and started an empire of his own. His son, Jim Mapes would soon take over the Mapes ranch and livestock which would put him in the history books as one of the cattle barons of Lassen County. Jim had worked for cow buyers for $12.00 a month and board and room. He was promoted to cow boss and his wages were raised to $15.00 a month. When Jim's father Ira died Jim bought the ranch from the Mapes Estate. He now was his own boss, and had to furnish his own board and room.

Jim started building on to the ranch and adding acreage and cattle. The original 160 acre portion of the ranch was the Brubaker place when his Uncle George had bought it. Then it belonged to McKezick then Mapes.

The Great Depression Hit! The bottom fell out of everything and the ranchers along with everyone else lost their entire holdings.

"Dad lost it all". That is how Julian Mapes describes the depression of the 1930's. Julian tells how he was a young boy and wanted to go on a rabbit drive. A box of shells cost ninety cents and it took Julian six months to pay it off. Jim Mapes didn't have any money for two or three years. He didn't even have a check book. The Winfield Banks had closed.

The hired help on the ranch worked for their room and board and took I.O.U's for their wages. They had no choice. They were lucky to have a bed and food to eat. As Julian tells it, they had to steal their own cattle to eat. The bank held the mortgage on all of the cattle and they belonged to the bank. Even though they carried the diamond J brand of the Mapes ranch, they had no right to them. The family had to eat and even though it was by rights their own beef that they were butchering, it was stealing as the cows belonged legally to the bank.

When the depression was finally over and the hired men collected their back wages, some of them were wealthy men.

The Reconstruction Finance Corporation was formed to bail the farmers and ranchers out of their debts. It was the forerunner of the Farm Credit Systems. With their financing Mapes was able to pick up and go on with the cattle business.

Jim Mapes was running 800 to 1,000 head of cattle. They just turned them loose in the spring and let them roam and graze the hills. There was no fences and no Forest Service or Bureau of Land Management in that area to control the ranchers and tell them what to do.

During the depression the bank allowed Jim Mapes $300.00 to run his business on for the entire year.

Julian started riding with the cowboys when he was nine years old. Every morning was a rodeo with the rank horses the cowboys started out with. Every day was exciting and Julian learned a lot. A lot of Indians worked on the Mapes ranch and they taught Julian to rope and ride.

Julian needed to make a little spending money so he ran a trap line. He trapped muskrats, skunks and anything that had hair on it. He saved his money all except a little bit he spent on the girls. The reward in the end of all the trapping and skinning paid off in getting Julian started in the cow business.

Young Julian went over near Eagle Lake to the Spalding tract deer hunting. Old Sam Webb had eight head of cattle. Sam wanted to move into Susanville, but could not because he had his few head of cattle to take care of. He offered to sell the cattle to Julian for $350.00 for all eight head and give him a horse to drive them home on. This would free Webb of his responsibilities. Julian had his savings from the trapping so he took Webb up on the deal and went home without a deer, but the young fifteen year old Julian had his start in the cattle business. He said he was a speculator from then on. From skunk hides to cattleman, what a switch.

Some of the neighbors and families that Julian can remember and school mates from the Litchfield area were McClelland, Baily, Humphreys, Marr, Bottoms, Wemple, Dill, Gibson, Johnson, Levitz, McAllister, Theodore, DeWitt, Fleming and Moulten.

Julian finished school at Lassen High School at Susanville and worked on the ranch for his father. He then enrolled in University of Nevada at

A Mapes Ranch cattle drive along Eagle Lake.

Reno and studied Animal Husbandry and Economics and graduated in 1939, ATO, Alpha Beta Omega and in the Phi Kappa Phi Honor Society.

While attending college, but home working on the ranch for vacation, Julian's Dad had sent him out to Grasshopper Valley to get a beef for the hay crew. While stopping at the water trough along the road another man stopped by and he and Julian visited. The man was from Reno and invited Julian to come have dinner with his family when Julian went back to college. The man had a daughter he wanted Julian to meet. Julian kept the dinner invitation and met his future wife. Julian Mapes and Evelyn Megliavacca were married in 1940.

Julian and his wife Evie have three daughters, Sally, Judy and Susan.

After marriage Julian stayed and worked for his Dad on the Mapes Ranch. Jim would give Julian a calf now and then and he had his herd of cows and their increase that he had bought from Sam Webb. His cow herd was almost up to fifty head. Jim wasn't charging Julian for any cow expense and his cows were ranging with his Dad's, so he had a good profit.

After the depression Lassen County found themselves to be nearly broke and holding thousands of acres that they had taken back when people could not pay their taxes. The county needed to get this property off of their hands and back on the tax rolls. Jim Mapes bought thousands of acres of this delinquent property for only five cents an acre. It was good grazing land, but not good for much else. At that time Jim was running about 1,000 head of cows and they were worth about $50.00 a head.

Julian stayed on the ranch for several years, but there came a time that he and his dad did not agree on the running of the Mapes Ranch and Julian decided it was time for him to move on. He felt Jim was running the ranch into the ground.

Julian and Evie moved to Eureka, California where Julian ran the county farm for Humboldt County. Julian enjoyed his job in Eureka and never regrets one hour that he spent there.

Julian's mother, Donna Mapes had been sickly for quite some time and she died when she was in her 50's.

In 1934 Tony and Percy Avilla, sheepmen from the southern valley owned 10,000 acres of grazing land from Hayden Hill, south. They wanted out and offered it to Jim Mapes for $200,000.00 for the entire acreage. A tidy sum of $20.00 an acre.

Another good deal that Mapes made was the banker wanted Jim to buy some range near Bogard that would run 500 head of cattle. Jim told the banker that he had no money. The bank had foreclosed on this property and could only hold it for so long. The banker offered it to Mapes for a total of $20,000.00 for the whole thing with no interest and no payments for ten years. The offer was too good to turn down.

Julian said he went back and forth each year on this range and spent thirty days a year in the rocks sleeping on top of them or between them whichever suited you. Just he and his pack horse and saddle horse tended the cattle and moved them. Julian said it was a good range until the Forest Service got control of it and they just ruined it.

1933 was the first year Mapes took their steers to Grasshopper Valley to put them on pasture. They had leased pasture from Mr. Heath. Jim had five hundred steers in the Avilla field. He had some pretty poor cowboys working for him and what Julian called drug store cowboys. The cowboys were sent to gather the steers, but came in with only two hundred. The next day Julian and some good cowboys went out and found the rest of the steers. Good help was hard to find.

Riding for cattle was different then than now, the day of the horse trailers. When gathering cattle in the fall you would ride out fifteen miles, gather the cattle and drive them home. It took 300 to 400 miles of driving to get the cattle all out to their ranges by the first of June. It made for tough horses and tougher cowboys.

When gathering cattle in the Fall you would ride out fifteen miles, gather the cattle and drive them home. Some times this would be a daily ritual for several days in a row. Some of the longest drives they would have cow camps along the way and make their base camp there or farther up the trail. They used a lot of pack horses before the days of the pick-up trucks.

Some of the cattle were impossible to find and some wintered out in the milder winters. But when the water all froze up the cows would drift home to the ranch and the hay pile. At that time there were not all the fences to keep the cattle from getting back to their home ranch.

In 1958 Jim Mapes died at the age of 82 years. Julian was working at Eureka at the time. A good friend and neighbor, Pierce McClelland took over and ran the Mapes ranch until Julian could tie up loose ends and get moved over from Eureka.

Jim had been using some bad judgement and making some bad investments and was running the Mapes ranch into the ground. Jim was as active as he could be at his age, but was over protective of his ranch and would not give up or let anyone help him make any decisions.

When Julian started running the Mapes ranch he hired all the haying done by a contractor. He owned no equipment except and old John Deere tractor.

Julian had to go to the bank to borrow money to run the Mapes ranch on and buy hay. The banker asked what Julian was going to use for collateral. He told the banker he was looking at him, meaning Julian was hoping to go on his good name. The banker wasn't quite sure he could go for that. The young cattleman told him, "those are your cows, and they have to eat". This gave the banker a completely different outlook of the situation. Jim Mapes had just about bankrupt the Mapes ranch, now it was up to Julian to put the ranch back on a positive track.

Cattle were going up in price. A good cow with a good calf were worth $250.00 a pair. The banks became more liberal in their lending.

Julian had become good friends of Mr. Heath that owned Grasshopper Valley. Julian leased pasture from Heath and made money both for himself and Heath. With the help of Mr. Heath's financing and Bank Of America Julian made the Mapes ranch one of the largest ranches in Northern California. Cattle with the "Diamond J" brand ran the ranges from Freedonyer Pass to Hayden Hill. The Mapes Ranch consisted of 22,000 acres owned and 30,000 acres rented along with Forest Service and Bureau of Land Management Permits. The ranch was scattered for 100 square miles. and 4,000 head of cattle wore the Mapes brand. Julian only had five hired men and they took care of the work and Julian took care of the financing and the books.

One time the Forest Service kept telling Julian that he had one steer on the range. He sent his cowboys out several times to try to find the critter. Time and time again they would look for him and the Forest Service kept complaining. Finally Julian handed a gun to the Forest Ranger, and said, "Next time you see that steer, shoot him, it would be cheaper that me chasing two men and equipment and horses all over the range to find him". The ranger said he couldn't do that, so Julian told him he didn't want to hear another word about it.

Another time Mapes had to drive the cattle from Pine Creek to the Avilla field. It was after the grazing season and a twenty-five mile, two day drive. The forest service complained that the cattle were grazing along the way. Julian told them it was pretty hard to keep a cow from eating when the grass was in front of them.

The water trough along the highway to Susanville is close to the home site where Julian and Evelyn Mapes now live. The old water trough was built to water the freight teams when they were hauling freight in 1920 and 21 to build the Eagle Lake tunnel. The tunnel is two and a half miles long and was an engineering miracle in those days. The 320 acres that Mapes bought there for a cow camp was purchased for $1,500.00 from Emerson's. At one time the Conklin's lived there. It was a stop over for travelers. Conklin's had a sawmill nearby. Now, a set of round corrals built with logs that Julian built when he was a young man stands ready to be used when needed. The only sign of the old Conklin cabin is a tall ancient poplar tree that gave shade to the pioneers.

A little further up the narrow graveled road is the beautiful home of Julian and Evie. Tall ceilings with many windows as Julian wanted to bring the outside in. A mountain lion had visited them the night before and was climbing on their roof. There was a rooster crowing in the yard, so the big cat hadn't gotten all of the chickens.

Julian had run the Mapes ranch, a corporation with his brother and sister. He had a lot of fun raising all of those cows, but the time had come for him to think of other things.

When the Carter administrating took office in Washington D.C. Julian knew it was time to get out. He knew he could not afford the high interest rates that Carter was putting in to effect. Sixteen to eighteen per-cent would bankrupt the Mapes ranch if they had to pay that kind of interest on their cattle loans.

Julian's daughters had not courted cowboys and they had others interests. He had a nephew, Larry Moulten that he hoped would be interested in taking over the ranch, but it didn't seem to work out that way.

1978. Top L. to R.: Some Lassen County Cattlemen; Frank Hagata, Julian Mapes, Leo Chappius, Ed Woods, Gene Rowland. Seated L. to R.: Frank Flux, Bud Price, Claude Wemple, Dick Tangeman.

Julian Mapes.

The home ranch was still at Litchfield and Julian and Evie had moved to their retirement home on the old Conklin place. Julian called up Jack Swickard and asked him if he would be interested in buying the Mapes Ranch. Jack didn't take long in making up his mind. The 22,000 owned acres, 30,000 rented and the 4,000 Mapes cows would soon change hands. In 1977 almost twenty years after Julian came to run his families estate thirty-eight deeds of trust changed hands and the Mapes ranch was run by the Swickard family. Julian still kept busy with the ranch helping the new owners as much as he could. He was not a man to sit idle.

Going back to take college classes and taking piano lessons were some of his accomplishments. A hunting trip to Kenya, Africa was a chance in a lifetime for the cattleman and a tanned hide of a zebra hangs on his office wall to remind him of the excitement he had there.

Julian likes to tell the story of when Swickard and Mapes had a couple thousand calves on pasture at the Concord Naval parcels. There were two brands on the calves, the diamond J of Mapes Corporation and the Five Dot of the Swickard Corporation. The Lieutenant was questioning the cowboy who was herding the cattle. He said, "I see you have two brands on your calves, how do you tell them apart"? The cowboy explained that some had a smooth brisket and some had a brisket waddle. The young Lieutenant watched as the calves trailed up the hill, "Oh, yes, I can see, some of those cattle do waddle". The cowboy laughed so hard he could hardly sit on his horse.

Julian can remember in 1950 when he ran for county supervisor. He said he must not have been a very good politician. He was a member of the DeMolay's, went through the offices of the Mason's, President of the Cattlemen and Farm Bureau. But now he enjoys a good book and his music and is still studying to keep his interests up and for entertainment. His theory is that a man should have three rewards in life .

A good dog, a good horse and a good woman. But not necessarily in that order.

Glorianne Weigand
June 16, 1995

Gerig house, taken in 1904.

Quite a Life

My hair is white and I am almost blind,
The days of my youth are far behind,
My neck is stiff, I can't turn my head,
Can't hear one half that is being said,
My legs are wobbly, can hardly walk,
But glory be I surely can talk,
My joints are stiff, won't turn in their socket,
And nary a dime do I have in my pocket.
But still I do have a lot of fun,
My heart with joy is over run,
I have friends—so kind and sweet,
And many more I'll never meet
So take from me and don't forget,
I'm still a livin and I ain't dead yet

The above poem was written by Peter Gerig Sr. of Bieber Lassen County, California on his 1923 Underwood typewriter for his 100th birthday. Peter, better known as Pete was born on the family ranch April 18, 1893 and was the tenth of eleven children.

Pete's father William Gerig was born in Wassen, Switzerland in 1847. William left home at the age of twelve and became self supporting. He went to France, where he worked on a goat farm. As he was entering his teens, he emigrated to the United States. The fourteen year old young man worked as a deck hand on a boat to pay for his passage to the New World. Young Gerig landed in New York, but this was not the life he wanted. Being a country boy at heart and hearing of the unclaimed west he boarded another boat and came to California by the way of the Isthmus of Panama, which was a five month trip.

In San Francisco he worked on the waterfront until he finally got the opportunity to work on a dairy farm in the Sacramento Valley, where he learned a through knowledge of dairying. William worked on the dairy farm for ten years, learning the business first hand.

The young Gerig worked hard and saved his money and when he was twenty-four years old he decided he wanted a place of his own. William rode north and came to Lassen county in 1871. Here he promptly preempted 160 acres of land that took in the southwest corner of the town of Bieber.

William met and married Sarah E. Carmichael in 1872. Sarah was the daughter of Moses A. Carmichael and Martha Jane (Gordon) Carmichael. The family came to California in 1870 across the plains from Iowa. Moses, Martha and their four children, Sarah, Allan, Calista and Mattie made the long hard trip in a covered wagon pulled by four oxen. Moses and his family settled on a homestead several miles west of Lookout. Here he built a sawmill that was water powered by a huge water wheel. The saw blade went up and down to cut the lumber. This was the first sawmill in the valley and was operated for over a quarter of a century.

William built a new home for his bride. He and his cousin Antone Gerig built the first two permanent homes in Bieber.

Homestead of Moses Carmichael at the sawmill. L. to R.: Moses Carmichael, William Gerig, Sarah (Carmichael) Gerig, Allen Carmichael, Martha Carmichael, and Calista Carmichael (in door).

William had built up quite a dairy herd and was farming and milking his cows at his farm in Bieber. (This homestead of Gerig's took in the property that the Bieber post office now sits on). Sarah and William started their family of eleven children. William born 1873, Lena 1875, Nancy 1878, Millie 1880, Charles 1882, Henry (died in childhood), Emma 1886, Eatha (died in infancy), Bertha 1891, (still living and will be 104 in August) Peter 1893 (is 102) and Keturah, 1895 (who passed away in 1995 at 99 years of age).

In 1890 William sold his homestead in Bieber to Agustas Smith who was also running the livery stable. William bought 600 acres two miles north of Bieber and moved his family there. The previous owner was Mr. Wolferson. There was a rickety two story house and one shed on the ranch. There were no barns. William had Dave Watson build two new barns for him.

The family lived in the old house until they tore it down in 1902 and a new two story home was built to take its place. This is the home that Pete Gerig still lives in today.

Eight children were born at Bieber and three were born on their new ranch.

Sarah and William raised dairy cows, beef cows, chickens, hogs, goats and horses. Part of the ranch was acquired under the swamp act of 1841 in which the government gave land to ranchers that were willing to drain it and make it productive.

In the winter of 1879-80 the snow came early and fell deep, much too deep for the cattle to dig down to the fall grass. William began to feed early, snow fell again as spring approached, and spring did not come until late May. He had fed most of his hay by then and most of his cattle had died. The Gerigs had even emptied their hay stuffed mattresses to try to save the cows, but it did little good. One milk cow was saved.

This was discouraging but William found that every farmer had suffered as much or more than he. He had a lot of hides from the dead cattle, which he sold. He worked hard and long and prospered enough to buy more land.

The Gerigs would take their cattle to Modoc County near Stonecoal along the Pit River to Gerig Camp in May and June. They would stay there and milk the cows and make cheese. The canyon was cool and there were lush green meadows for the cattle to graze. The cheese was made into large twenty pound rounds and wrapped in cheese cloth to cure. The butter was packed in firkins (small wooden tubs),then covered in brine. In the cool weather of the fall it was time to take their dairy products to market. Sarah would wash the butter and work out the salt and brine and wrap it in one and two pound loafs and fresh cloth. The wagons were loaded with fifty rounds of cheese weighing twenty pounds each and all of the butter they had made. A load was taken to Redding to McCormick and Seltzer Company and either sold, but most of the time was traded for dry goods or food staples. Some times the cheese and butter was hauled to Carson City, Nevada.

In July the family would move back to the ranch to start to put up the hay for their winter feed.

The haying was done with mowing machines and buck rakes and stacked by hand. Six teams would be used in the fields to mow and rake the hay. Six foot derrick forks, then nets were used to raise the hay to the top of the stack by the derrick. There, the stackers would move the loose hay pitchfork by pitchfork full to make huge neat tall stacks. Pete was proud of the neat tall stacks he put up. He liked the sides straight and smooth and he was good at his job.

William died of pneumonia in 1898 when he was only fifty-one years old. Pete was only five years old. Sarah was left with all the children and a mortgage on the ranch. At that time there was no government help and times were hard for the Gerig family. Sarah was determined and with the help of the older children went on. Will was twenty-five years old and most of the responsibility was heaped on his shoulders. There were no luxuries, they were happy to just have food and clothes.

The Gerig children walked the two miles to Bieber to school and home again each day. Only in the very deep snow were they taken by sleigh with one of the older children driving the team.

One time Pete and his younger sister Keturah, (Turrie) played hookey for two weeks. They would leave for school with their lunch pails, but would spend the days playing in the fields and the ditches. Turrie got awful sunburned, and Pete says he doesn't know why they did it. One day their older sister ran into the teacher in town and the teacher, Paul Hopper asked why the children hadn't been attending school? Pete says, "Boy when we got home did we ever get a blastin".

After the death of William the dairy cows dwindled down and were replaced with beef cows, so the ranch was now more of a cattle ranch than a dairy ranch.

Sarah suffered a great deal with arthritis and rheumatism. Her hands became quite crippled. A Chinese doctor came to the valley and treated her with herbs, which gave her some relief.

Pete went away to the Imperial Valley to business college. He got his diploma in 1911 and got a job sitting up the business books for a store. He worked at that job for two weeks and decided he wanted to go back to the ranch in Northern California. Pete went one year to Chico to

Guy Moss, Frank Gerig, Pete Gerig and Charlie Gerig.

college, but other than that he has spent his entire 102 years on the same ranch he was born on.

School held some very fond memories for Pete. His very best friend was Aubrey Bieber who he had gone to grade school with. Aubrey was as short as Pete was tall and they were often times called Mutt and Jeff. They were as close as any two men could be until Aubrey passed away a few years ago.

Pete can recall in 1910 and 1911 driving cattle from Big Valley to the Gage Ranch near Chico, Calif. It took five cowboys fourteen days to make the long drive then they had to ride back home again. Cale Guthrie, Lee West, Tom Pratt and Ralph Oilar were the cowboys making the drive with Pete. Ralph Oilar was the one to drive the lead cow for the two year old steers to follow. One year they lost one steer and the next year they found him grazing along the trail so took him on to Chico with them.

On May 1, 1914 at Pittville, California Leona Day and Peter Gerig were married by Virgil Vineyard in a home of friends there. Pete and Leona honeymooned at McArthur during a May Day celebration that was an annual event then. They returned to their new Big Valley home by horse and buggy. They moved in to the bunk house on the ranch near Sarah. Leona was from Little Hot Springs Valley. Leona's family were pioneers there in that little corner of Modoc County that now is know as Day. Leona was born in 1896 on the family homestead there. The settlement was named after her grandfather as he was one of the first to settle there. Mr. Day sent for his son Samuel Day and his wife Anna to move up from Colusa to take up the homestead adjoining him. Samuel

In front of Hank Carlies Saloon in Bieber. Pete Gerig driving. Aubrey Bieber in back.

Leona and Pete's wedding picture, 1914.

and Anna had six children in their family. Jim, Nathanial, Cecil, Frances, Mable and Leona. Leona went to school at McArthur until 1909. That year her father passed away and she went to live with an older brother and his wife. In 1911 Anna Day remarried Dave Anderson and moved to Bieber to run the Livery Stable and Leona came with them. She finished her school in Bieber. A highlight of her life was to be chosen Goddess of Liberty for a fourth of July celebration in 1913.

Leona pitched right in and made herself a part of the Gerig ranch. Raising a big garden, cooking for a crew of fifteen men, raising bummer lambs, chickens, turkeys and helping with the cattle were all of the jobs she helped with.

The year of 1918 was so dry. There was no water in the Pit River that runs through the meadows of the Gerig ranch. They drove all their cattle to Cottonwood and sold most of them there. Pete and Leona went down to care for the remainder of the cattle and Sarah and Turrie stayed home to keep the home fires burning.

In the early days Bieber was quite a little town. There was a dance hall above the livery stable and dances were held every Saturday night. Pete and Leona never missed a dance. When that building burned down there would be dances in the Dance Land Hall or at Punkin Center.

The livery stable had been run by Leona's stepfather Dave Anderson. Nathan Bieber had a store, Mr. Rudee had a store that was run by John Leventon. Jim Summers and Oscar Holcomb ran the Corner Saloon, Hank Carlies had a saloon, Durfee ran the Post Office and a harness shop in the back. The I.O.O.F. Hall was upstairs. Brownells ran a hotel and Andy Babcock had a blacksmith shop. Jim Levitt was the Sheriff and Alvin Holcomb was the Deputy.

Leona and Pete had two sons, Norris born in 1916 and Harold born 1919, (he died in 1927 at the age of eight).

When Sarah Gerig passed away in 1926 the ranch was left as an estate and Pete and Leona purchased it from his brothers and sisters in 1929.

In 1929 hard times hit and then the great depression. The Gerigs lost almost everything. The bank had a mortgage on the cattle and had threatened to foreclose. Pete and Leona did anything to make a dollar to get by. Fat steers at that time sold for three and one-half cents a pound.

A cheese factory was built at Bieber. It was a cooperative owned by a group of the farmers in the area. Hugh Watson ran the creamery and cheese factory. This was a big help to the dairymen. Gerigs along with all the others no longer had to make their own butter and cheese and haul it for hundreds of miles with their team and wagons to market it. They only had to take their fresh milk and cream to town and have it processed there.

In 1920 Pete Gerig a dedicated Republican was voted in as Lassen County Supervisor, a position he held for twenty-eight years. One of Pete's main projects was the paving of the seventy miles of graveled road between Bieber and the Lassen County seat of Susanville. When Pete first started as county supervisor he would sometime have to make the trip horseback which was several days round trip. Other times he went horseback to Alturas, then boarded the NCO train to Amadee then on to the Courthouse in Susanville by stagecoach. Then retraced his route back to Bieber.

Pete also worked hard and diligently on trying to get the Allen Camp Dam built on Pit River. At one time they were so close to building it that Pete could almost visualize the water running over the huge dam between Canby and Lookout. Many trips to Washington D.C. and meeting after meeting, but there was always an obstacle somewhere along the line. Years and years later they are farther away than ever in getting the dam built that is so badly needed to preserve water.

Twenty years on the Lassen planning commission and twenty-four years on the resource board are also added to Pete's remarkable list of accomplishments. Over fifty years in public service is a big achievement for any man. Pete's list reads along with other things V.P. of the Northern Five Counties Association, director of the Shasta-Cascade Wonderland Association, trustee of the Bieber school board, foreman of the Lassen County Grand Jury, President of the Big Valley Historical Society, the Elks Lodge and the California Automobile Association, also added to the list was that he was on the 1939 World's Fair committee.

Pete can remember buying his first Blue Oldsmobile in the early 1900's. He bought it at Redding, Calif. for $500.00, "it was an Oakland", Pete added.

Pete recalls, I wasn't much of a leader of organizations, I belonged to 'em, but I didn't care about the leadership. I think leadership wears people out faster. I was in a dozen public offices, but I didn't make any waves, I just went along. I always wanted to duck out of being the head of anything because I was trying to run a ranch".

Pete has the largest scrap book anyone ever saw. It is an old fabric sample book from 1901. He has glued hard and fast his total life in his "BOOK".

Everything from poems he has written, every newspaper clipping, an American flag and letters and personal autographed pictures from U.S. Presidents Nixon, Ford, Reagan and Bush. As Pete refers to the gigantic book, he says, "this is my life, it is all in here".

Gerig like his mother before him is a Republican through and through. As far as he is concerned there is no other political party. When asked if

W.H. Gerig Family L. to R.: Emma, Charles, Millie, Will, Keturah, Pete, Lena.

he ever voted for a democrat, he said, only once, I voted for Congressman Bizz Johnson, he was a mighty fine man."

In 1935 Norris married Dorothy Brewster from Dana. They have two children, Peter who married Lynne Flournoy and Glenda who married John Solus.

Pete and Leona retired in 1962 and rented the ranch to their son Norris and his wife Dorothy. They still lived in their big two story home on the ranch helping out whenever they could.

1973 was a memorable time as Pete was named "Old Timer of The Year", at the Lassen County Fair. An event he rarely missed. Leona was named InterMountain Cowbelle of The Year". Leona was photographed by the local newspaper displaying one of the beautiful quilts she had made. She was very proud of the honor.

Leona that had stood by the side of this pillar of a man for sixty-one years passed away in 1975.

The Gerig ranch goes on with four generations living and working on the ranch, Pete, Norris, Peter and his son Bryan.

The Hereford cattle graze the meadows when they are not on the Forest Service or Bureau of Land Management allotments or being fed in the winter time. Some of the cattle are wintered near Redding.

Peter and his sister Glenda started a 4-H project of registered Herefords that they purchased from Floyd Bidwell in 1950. The ranch still maintains the registered herd, but they do not sell as many bulls as they use to.

Pete, not wanting to live alone in his golden years married a widow friend that he had gone to school with. Eighty-three year old Pete and Beulah Raber were married in 1976. Beulah remarkcd that they had gone to school together when Henry Ford was starting the Ford Motor Company and the Wright Brothers piloted their air craft at Kitty Hawk. Pete and Beulah were married by Pete's long time friend Judge Aubrey Bieber. It was the first wedding that the eighty-three year old Judge had ever performed. Being married to Beulah for almost twenty years, Pete is happy to say he has been happily married for almost eighty-one years.

Hunting and fishing has been a love for the rancher from Lassen county. He has hunted elk in Wyoming, Antelope in Nevada and shot a bear near Bartle, Calif. Pete hunted mule deer near the Gerig cow camp when bucks had horns that you could be proud of. Fishing on the Klamath River or at Eagle Lake was also enjoyed by this sportsman.

When Pete turned 100 Peter and Lynne wrote a poem about the things Peter remembers about his Grandfather.

A 100 years has come to pass,
And with each, comes the thought,
of all the happy memories that through the years you've wrought.
The hurting and the sad times have also been, I hope they have
tended to make us stronger men.
Trips and riding to every corner in Lassen and visiting and joking
along the way.
Quickly together we passed many a day.
The dented fender on the Ford, we got it fixed in a hurry.
Diaper the pony you got me, couldn't I make him scurry.
You taught me how to fish and hunt, on every outing the tag along
runt.
The camp out up at Roany Flat what great memories come to mind
from that.
A taste of teasing always came my way, made life then, fun and gay.
Tall in stature like a tree, you've been a special man to me.
Happy 100th Birthday Gramp 1893-1993.

This gentle man now enjoys his life in retirement. He said he has done it all. His two grandchildren, five great grandchildren and nine great, great grandchildren enjoy visiting him and listening to his stories.

The legacy of the Gerig Ranch with the PG brand on their cattle is owned and operated by Norris and Dorothy, Peter and Lynne. Pete's great grandson Bryan also works on the ranch.

Pete Gerig says the worst thing that could happen to him now is to die when a democratic president is in office in Washington D.C.

Pete remarks as he settled back in his chair ready for a nap, Quite a life, Quite a life.

Glorianne Weigand
July 15, 1995

Pete and Leona on their 60th wedding anniversary.

116

The Beautiful Dixie Valley

Way up North where the cold wind blows, the pavement ends and the West begins is a beautiful little valley known as Dixie Valley. In Northern California in a little corner of Lassen county lies one of the largest ranches in the northwest. Once a large Indian reservation and known as Dixie Swamp it was the home of many Indians and wild animals is now one large ranch owned by John Crook.

Dixie was settled by the Reaves family. David and his wife Anna and his brothers Andrew, James and Thomas traveled from Illinois and settled in Dixie Swamp on April 1, 1873. There were other homesteaders, George Riddle, Rosco Gates and George Snaden. Each of the men had homesteaded one hundred and sixty acres at the West end.

Dixie is about eight miles long and a mile wide in places. Dixie Peak, Bald Mountain and Indian Mountain all tower over the valley. Indian Mountain was the lookout point for the Indians, from which they watched the white trespassers take over their hunting grounds and kill their game.

Horse Creek runs through the valley and is supplied by fifty springs besides Little Davis and Big Davis Creeks, Russell Dairy Creek and Indian Creek. The water is used to irrigate the lush meadows of the ranch then wanders on to join the Pit River. Dixie Swamp was so named because it had poor drainage and tulle marshes. Good management was practiced by the land owners and the swamps were drained and turned into productive hay meadows and pastures.

The Reaves Brothers raised sheep, cattle and running horses which foaled in Dixie and were sent to Chico to be trained and raced.

David Reaves built the big white two story house which has been a Dixie landmark since its creation in 1890. The large house was the home of the owners and mangers and the cookhouse and dining rooms for the men. In the early days there was a dining room for the white cowboys and ranch hands and an Indian dining room for the Indian cowboys and ranch hands. They later tore the Indian dining room off of the house and had only the one dining room with its long white oilcloth covered table the full length of the room and the white painted benches for the men to sit on at each side. The table was fully sit with all plates and cups upside down in case the places were not all filled at a certain meal this would keep them clean until they were needed. The house had twelve rooms, screened in porches and a large cold room and cellar.

The original furniture in the house was sent by wagon from Illinois. Written on the back of one piece of a marble topped dresser was the address of Fitzwater Company, Fall City, Calif.

The blacksmith shop built by the Reaves still stands today and is used for shoeing horses. It is built of logs, wooden pegs and square nails. Many branding irons that were forged and hand shaped in that shop are burned into the walls of the shop. A sign above the door reads, Reaves Shop 1873.

Reaves built many rock sheep corrals and they are still in existence today between Dixie and Coyote Canyon. Reaves ran five bands of sheep.

The Reaves brothers had good running horses and had great faith in them. They had one horse, Dixie Bell that they thought could not be beat. They took the mare to Canada to race and placed a large bet on her. The horse was good, but there was one that was better and Dixie Bell came in second. The Reaves brothers lost also, and lost their ranch because they had bet so much on one horse.

According to records at the Lassen County Court House, Dixie was sold to C.W. and Philomen Clarke on April 27, 1892. The transaction included 2,320 acres of mostly swampland and rock fences built by the Indians. In 1906 the ranch was incorporated to C.W. Clarke Co. of San Francisco, Calif.

Later the Clarke Co. purchased a Big Valley ranch that had thousands of acres and a large swamp. This ranch was later sold to the W.H. Hunt Estate, (it now belongs to the Dept. of Fish and Game). They also bought the Murdock Ranch near Pittville and changed the name to Beaver Creek Ranch. This was the site of a large Indian battle.

James Snell was the superintendent for Clarke. He purchased acres of government land and many Indian allotments. Some of the Indians kept their land and stayed at Dixie while others moved to a new location.

James and his wife Zella lived on the Beaver Creek Ranch. There transportation was horse and buggy. As the old cowboys told the story, Snell was driving C.W. Clarke into Dixie with his black buggy and team. As they crossed the divide between Little Valley and Dixie, C.W. looked out across the big open valley. "Jim", he asked, "Isn't it too early to have so many cattle in the fields?" "Mr. Clarke," Jim answered smiling, those are horses." C.W. raised his voice above the clatter of the wheels. "Jim, get those horses out of Dixie". The large band of mares and foals, mostly left over from the Reaves' band, took the long trail to the Warner Mountains in Modoc County, many miles to the north. They were left there to run wild. Bays, buckskins and roans, a good looking bunch of horses. They were left to roam the wild and in breed and were classed as mustangs.

Clarke used the "Lazy Q" iron on the cattle and the "HS" on the horses. Clarke ran around five thousand head of cattle, several work horses to do the ranch work and many saddle horses. Mares were only used to produce foals and never to be ridden.

Dixie was remote and at the end of a graveled road. Groceries had to be hauled from Fall City, (now known as Fall River Mills), a sixty mile round trip with team and wagon.

Dixie was a lively place, beside the big white house there were two bunk houses. One for the Indian men and one for the white men. A store, spring house, blacksmith shop, two barns, smokehouse, sheep sheds, and a machinery shed.

A mail service was tried for three months from Pittville, Leigh Vernon was the pony express rider. There was not enough demand for the service, so it was stopped.

The Indians were hired in summer months to hay the big fields and stack the loose hay by hand. They brought their families, teams and many dogs. They pitched their tepees and tents near Dixie Springs west of the house. The horses were turned loose in a small pasture. The camp came alive with booze, gambling, tepee creeping and fights, some with knives. When Fall came and the snow started to fall they headed for their homes, Hat Creek, Grasshopper Valley, Big Valley and Fall River. Some had their permanent homes in Dixie. You could tell winter was on the way when the large caravan of covered wagons, buggies and horseback riders headed out of the valley. There were about thirty families, plus all the dogs and a few little foals trailing along behind.

Some of the foremen for the Clarke Co. who rode those big good looking geldings the company raised were Charley Carlton, Crawford Clarke, Bill Vineyard, Charley Whitney, Perry Sutton, Charley Snell and James Snell.

After James Snell passed away in 1930 Edwin Owens was superintendent. Bill Denio and I.C. McCall were some of the foremen on the ranch.

Hay foremen were called straw bosses and a few that had the honor of that job were Elmer Williams, Tracy Hines, George Farmer, Henry Heaton, Melvin Stevenson, and Evan Guttry. Some of their wives did the cooking for the hay crews.

Cow bosses were Leonard Johnson,, Roy Swain, Elmer Williams and George Corder.

After C.W. Clarke died his daughter took over the reins of the ranch. A grandson was manager for a time.

Weird things have happened in Dixie. Around 1899 Charley Carlton was the foreman and well liked by all the ranch hands.

Charley had hired a chinaman cook. The chinaman also milked the cows. Carlton overheard the cowboys talking that the cook was going to poison Carlton's food. When the chinaman came back from the barn carrying two buckets of milk early the next morning, Charley was waiting by a small gate and hit the chinaman over the head with a wagon spoke and killed him. The chinaman is buried out on Chinaman Knob south of Dixie. There are also eight Indian graves on the same knob.

Sie Elliott, Leonard Johnson and Dick McGrue were some of the great mustangers and real cowboys. Jeff Eades, a half-breed Indian worked off and on for the Dixie outfit for many years. He was also a wild horse runner, roper, rawhide worker and silver smith. He and his wife Martha lived in their little house on the Dixie ranch for many years. Jeff used a sixty foot reata and rode a slick-forked saddle. Jeff passed on some of his talents to some of the cowboys like Lee Crews that were interested in that sort of art work.

In 1908 Jeff and John Nelson from near Likely drove one hundred and thirty horses down the Sacramento Valley to Petaluma. They would cut fences and keep on going, picking up more horses on the way. The trip took about two weeks. At Petaluma they picked out sixty head of big horses and put them on a ferry and went to San Francisco where they spent the winter breaking the horses to work.

Some of the old time cowboys that rode in the Dixie country ran in to the hundreds, some of the most memorable were Dick and Ned McGrue, Aubrey Vestal, Aubrey Burton, Keith Burton, Frank Bartle, Troy Fitzwater, Arch Hollenbeak, Billy Blake, Leigh Vernon, George Farmer and John Gerig. Some of the Indian cowboys were, Nelson Johnson, Billy Phillips, Ramsey Blake, Lyman LaMarr, Ike and Bob Reaves and Ed Johnson.

Some of the later cowboys who rode the Dixie horses were John Brooks, Jim Short, Sie Elliott, Ed Ivory, Clarence Rice, Lester Haynes, Leonard Johnson, Roy Swain, George Corder, Clark Hall and many more.

Clarke Company had many cooks, men and women, some were good and stayed for a time, and others put the first meal on the table and packed their bags before the dishes were done. It was not an easy job with wood stoves to cook on and candles and kerosene lamps to light up the rooms.

Winters were so cold in Dixie that one cook did the cooking with her long wool coat on and her overshoes. The water freezing in the faucet before a meal could be prepared.

The blacksmiths Jim Johnson and later Roy Bassett kept busy keeping all the horses shod and the tools in repair.

An Indian school once stood across the valley by Big Davis Creek. The one room building was heated by a big wood burning stove, but still it was awful cold in the winter. The walls were lined with cardboard and paper of all kinds to keep the wind and snow out. In 1923 there were six white children attending the school and the rest were all Indian children.

There were several famous Indian tribal doctors in the Dixie area. Ida LaMarr and Hattie Johnson took care of the medicinal needs of their own people and many of their white friends.

Aubrey Vestal spent most of his young life in Dixie, strawboss in summer and feeding out the hay in winter. He, Charley Kidder and Ed Robinson spent two summers building the twelve miles of drift fence from Little Davis Creek to Jessen Canyon. Hazel Robinson was their cook in a chuck wagon pulled by two mules. At that time Aubrey said the Clarke company ran 5000 cows, one hundred horses and two mules.

Hack Lambert of Little Valley and Dale Swain also worked at Dixie in the early days. They leveled land at the upper end with teams and fresnos. They batched in a cabin and were paid $45.00 a month.

July 31, 1942 T.E. Tom Connolly of San Francisco purchased Dixie from the Clarke Company. Clarke had owned the ranch for fifty years. Tom was a contractor on the Pit One Powerhouse tunnel. A powerful and wealthy man that usually got what he wanted in life. In 1921 Tom drove a team and buggy into Dixie, and as he was leaving the valley he looked back and said, "Dixie Valley, I will own you some day", and his words came true.

Tom's wife Myrtle was not as delighted with his purchase as he was. The big two story white house standing by the cool spring was quite a sight. It was all painted a dark green on the inside and Mrs. Connolly soon changed that and sent most of the furniture to the dump and started to clean house.

Tom was cleaning house in another way of speaking, by firing the foreman and hiring Bill Vineyard as his top hand. Vineyard was soon replaced by Bill Spalding and his wife Hazel as the managers. The Spaldings ran a tight ship and soon Dixie Valley was a beautiful well groomed place that all could be proud of. Bill was an excellent foreman and got along well with all the men and was well respected. Hazel ran the house and the cooks with as much capability. Their two sons, Nelmer and Ernest worked on the ranch. When Tom bought the Loomis ranch in

Big Valley a few years later Nelmer and his family moved over the hill to run that ranch.

Mr. Connolly started to show improvements in the Dixie Valley. A 10,000 gallon propane tank was shipped in and the wood stoves were replaced. Six miles of new road was built to Little Valley. A meat cooling room, a new spring house and a grocery storage house were added. He moved in sixteen cabins from his Big Bend construction camp for bunk houses for all the men rebuilding Connolly's dream ranch and the ranch hands. Reservoirs were built, fences were built, machinery sheds and barns. Everything was going so fast.

Tractors, mowers, trucks, cats, pickups, trailers and anything he took a whim for was purchased and sent to Dixie to make it a more modern cow outfit.

Tom started buying the best Quarter Horses he could find and started quite a horse breeding project. Many of the Dixie Valley horses were used on the ranch and were consigned to many horse sales on the west coast.

Tom Connolly's Dixie Valley ranch was the eleventh largest Quarter Horse breeder in California. Some of the famous horses that Connolly owned were Poco Chip, Poco Bueno and Skipity Scoot.

Hack Lambert was working on the Dixie ranch for Bill Spalding. In 1946 Hack married Lil Bognuda. They moved to a little one room cabin and in 1947 they moved back to Little Valley where they lived in a two room cabin and Hack worked in the sawmill. At that time they never dreamed they would return to Dixie as the foreman and run this beautiful ranch.

In 1951 Mr. Connolly purchased a ranch west of Red Bluff for winter pasture. Harry Gilbert worked on the ranch there for many years. The Red Bluff ranch was 6,000 acres and a long ways from nowheres. The Dixie Valley ranch grew to 13,000 acres and the Big Valley ranch consisted of 4,000 acres.

In 1950 Hack Lambert went back to work for Dixie along with a couple of other excellent cowhands, Forest and Wad Carpenter, they were kept real busy breaking all the Dixie horses they could.

Tom Connolly was a Civil Engineer and had many projects building tunnels, dams and bridges that help to finance the project of his dream ranch.

Hack and Lil were spending the winters with the cattle in the valley. They always had horses there to break to keep them busy.

In 1955 Bill and Hazel Spalding retired and left Dixie after twelve years and moved to Susanville.

Bill Spalding with a Dixie Valley Buck.

Dixie Valley cowboys, L. to R.: Ernie Spalding, Will Spalding,
Jeff Eades, Lee Crews, Nelmer Spalding.

Lil Bognuda Lambert.

Everyone hated to see them go, the cook Selena LaMarr, Forest and Wad Carpenter and Byrel Wendt were left to run the Dixie Valley Ranch. Tom Connolly was tied up in court over some litigations and did not have time to tend to the ranch. The death of Mrs. Connolly left Tom with a large tax debt. Some property and many cattle had to be sold to satisfy this debt.

Joe DeMello an old rodeo cowboy was hired to take the foreman's job. He had a young lazy wife, a bottle problem and no idea on earth how to run a ranch. When Tom got out of court he went to Dixie and was heart sick. The Carpenter boys had quit, Selena no longer was seen in the kitchen and things were a wreck.

Tom Connolly went to Hack Lambert in August and asked him if he would run his cow outfit. The only thing I ask is for you to be honest with me. And as Lil put it Dixie Valley always had some characters and two more were just added to the pot.

July 17, 1966. Hack Lambert, Angelo Leoni, Tom Connolly.

The job wasn't easy, in the few short months that the Spaldings had been gone it seemed like things had really gone down hill. Hack and Lil had their job cut out for them and big shoes to fill. It takes guts, determination and a feeble mind to run a cow outfit in the North Country, where the elements knock on your gate each morning. When Selena LaMarr heard the Lamberts were looking for a cook she returned to keep the kitchen fires burning again.

The Dixie Valley cattle ranged the B.L.M. and Forest Service ranges and mingled with the cattle from Big Valley. The Big Valley ranchers would ride over the mountains in deep snow to gather the last straggling cattle. They would gather the Dixie strays on the way and take them to the ranch and spend the night there. Lil and Hack always enjoyed the company of Virgil Knudsen, Stan and Lawrence Weigand, Haskell and Jerry Parks, Jim and Mike Wayman, Floyd Walker and Bill Thompson. The cowboys were always thankful for the warm dry beds, good food and fun. They would visit and play cards late into the night and the cook would always make a big batch of candy for them to eat. Modoc County has its Devil's Gardens, but the range between Dixie Valley and Big Valley was "No Man's Land", and could be treacherous to ride.

Wendell Carpenter was breaking a few colts. A little gelding bucked him off, saddle, bridle and all. The bridle was still buckled up. Wendell got up, pushed the saddle off of his legs, picked up his bridle and said, "I'll be damned!" Wendell and his wife Rea were at Dixie for a time and Rea helped in the kitchen. Rea's brother Jack Monchamp also was riding at the ranch.

Winters were harsh in Dixie Valley and only the strong could survive. 1964 blew in with twenty inches of new snow on top of what they had and the thermometer registered eight degrees above zero. That was the high for several days. Equipment balked and wouldn't start so the cattle could be fed. Over a thousand cows, eighty bulls, some calves and a hundred head of quarter horses had to be fed, the cowboys hung up their spurs and helped get the hay to the cattle.

1973 Hack's famous last words were reality. He said every winter, I've spent my last winter in Dixie. Hack and Lil had bought a little place in Red Bluff and were ready to move to the warmer climate. Hack gave his notice to Tom and by Fall the Lamberts had made the move. As Lil put it, "Money or an oil well in Texas couldn't buy the memories of Beautiful Dixie Valley".

Byrel and Janelle Wendt took over the job of feeding cows and keeping Dixie going. Byrel was a right hand man and could do any job that had to be done.

Hack Lambert on Ginger Dan, 1970.

Hack and Lil Lambert, 1973.

In 1977 John Crook of San Francisco bought the famous Dixie Valley Ranch from the T.E. Connolly Estate. Crook was in the lumber business and had a race horse farm in Kentucky.

The remote ranch in Lassen County now had a new owner. Someone who was proud to own such a beautiful ranch with the Hereford cattle grazing the meadows and the Forest Service and Bureau of Land Management allotments. Someone who took pride in the white painted fences, barns and buildings. Crook was a good judge of excellent horses and cattle and wanted to run a top notch ranch. The ranch consisted of 15,000 deeded acres and 100,000 acres in grazing permits on the U.S. Forest Service and Bureau of Land Management.

Several couples took their turn at managing Dixie, Willis and Jenny Yates. Clifford and Kristin Cunningham, a local couple were there several months running the outfit. Rick Sanders was manager for a time.

In 1979 Rich and Mary O'Conner and their two children Gina and Rondo came from Montana to manage the ranch for Crook. The O'Conners were not totally new to the country as they were raised in Northern California. A busy place, with the huge dinning room table full most of the times. Mary did the cooking but had some help during the busiest times as she helped with the riding also.

Branding days were full of fun and a lot of hard work as a lot of fellow ranchers and friends came to help rope and brand the cattle.

Haying was contracted out as that saved on equipment costs and the hiring of extra men in the summer for that job.

Part of the cattle were sent to the winter range at Red Bluff, but some were still kept at the home ranch for the winter.

The O'Conners made Dixie Valley their home for ten years, watching the ranch prosper and grow. Gina and Rondo grew up roping and riding and being very good at it. In 1989 the ranch was put into the hands of a management agency and Rich and Mary moved on.

An employee of the management agency Mike Vehil and his wife Teri moved to Dixie Valley. It was a long way from no where for Teri, who had been raised on a dairy in southern California. Teri said she cried when she first saw her new home, but now she loves it in Dixie and can't imagine any where else she would rather raise her children.

Where the bunk houses once stood and the home of Jeff Eades is a double wide mobile home for the managers Mike and Teri. The big two story house of 1890 stands lonely waiting for a loving family to move in to it. It is used for a bunk house for some of the men and has been used for other families living there.

Things are busy at Dixie as usual, with haying, riding and the everyday ranch life. As Teri toured me through the old house I could remember the pies Selena had just taken out of the oven. In the barn the stall sign of Poco Chip still hangs over his stall. As I went with Mike to catch a couple of saddle horses in the corral with fifteen other horses we visited about the workings of the ranch that I have known most of my life. The things are not like they were in the good old days as some would like to remember them, but the spring of 1995 will not be one John Crook and Mike Vchil will soon forget.

It had been a long hard winter in the North country. Feed was short in the hills and the cattle had to come off the range early. The snows came early and the cows that were usually sent to Red Bluff to winter range had to be kept at the ranch in Dixie. It was too muddy to get the cattle trucks in to haul them out. Mike was not worried, he had enough hay to get him through a normal winter. But it was not a normal winter. It started snowing in November and kept it up. There was no let up and the cows consumed more hay than normal. It took a lot of feed for them to just keep in shape without the stress of calving. The fall calving cows were doing O.K. The spring calvers were across the valley up in the juniper trees.

On March 10, 1995 Mike woke up to the sound of rain. There had been a lot of snow in the hills before that, but now torrents of rain. As he noticed the north slopes of the mountains, they were bare and the meadow was flooding. His hay pile was getting short, but he had plans of buying some and having it brought in. He decided he had better go look at the culverts where the water was coming off of the hill at Horse Creek. It was on the ranch, and the only road into headquarters, but several miles away.. He drove up on one side and a neighbor Ted Crum was on the other side of the raging water. Ted told him, "Maybe you should leave a pickup on the other side in case you need to get to town if the water gets higher." Mike headed back to the ranch to get another man and a pickup. There were ten people at the ranch including a pregnant woman that was due any day. The men returned within twenty minutes to cross with the other pickup, just in time to see the culverts shooting out of the flooded road like torpedoes.

The phones were out, so Mike rode a saddle horse across the miles of flooded meadow through the mountains to the little village of Little Valley to phone for help and supplies. It was an all day trip and dark by the time he and his horse crossed the acres of flooded meadows back home.

He knew the cattle on the hill would be in trouble because he could not get feed from the ranch to them. 1500 head of cattle stranded in snow and no way to get hay to them because of bureaucracy.

By March 22 things were very serious with the cattle and more snow was falling. Mike called County Supervisors, Farm Advisors, Sheriff emergency personal, (no help was available for livestock.)

John Crook and Mike Vehil decided the closest haul for hay to the cattle would be to use a nearby Forest Service road and have the hay trucked in. A call to the Forest Service was made and the normal run around was activated. No one wanted to make a decision and everyone wanted to pass the buck. The Forest Service told the Dixie crew to think of other options. A truck load of hay was waiting and a contractor was

Mike Vehil, Manager of Dixie Valley and his daughter.

on hand to grade the snow off the road. But still a standstill. The cowboys only wanted to get hay to the cattle on the U.S.F.S. road, but not feed on it. The cows were on the Bureau of Land Management land and a call the that office in Alturas was made. The B.L.M. told them to do what they had to do and they would take care of the paper work later, but get feed to the cattle.

Red tape, regulations and paper work assisted in the death of around seventy head of Dixie cattle. The fault cannot be laid at any single door step, but it was a situation that should have never happened and all involved hopes it never happens again.

A helicopter was finally hired to drop the hay to the starving cattle. The helicopter also dropped groceries and supplies to the ranch families that were stranded.

The families had to boat back and forth across the washout for several months, until the water subsided enough so they could put an earth fill dam in it. This was a temporary thing until the culverts could be installed. But due to more red tape the culverts are not in and winter is on the way. If it is another wet winter and high water comes it might be a repeat of Spring 1995.

It seems so senseless that grown men and women, ranchers and Forest Service employees arguing over tearing up a road that the Dixie owner was willing to rebuild if necessary, while cattle lay starving and are too weak to get to the hay that had been air lifted to them.

Today, things have calmed down in Dixie to a busy gentle roar, but winter will soon be on its way. Teri and Mike Vehil and John Crook are hoping it is nothing like the last one they endured.

(Some of the early history of Dixie Valley was taken from a manuscript written by Lil Lambert. Permission was granted by her family to use it in this Dixie Valley story.)

Glorianne Weigand
August 18, 1995

Cedarville, California, 1880.
The home the Hill family
lived in (at left).

Grizzly Bears and Indian Attacks

Sagebrush, juniper trees, coyotes, mule deer and Indians were predominant in Modoc County in 1864 when brothers, Dan and Frank Hill came with their parents to Surprise Valley.

It had been a long trip from Iowa for the family. They came to this little corner of California to farm but decided to get in to the cattle business instead. Claiming a homestead just north of Cedarville and building their home and ranch was the first business at hand.

When Frank was nineteen years old he had a terrifying experience for a young man from the East. It would have been horrifying for anyone to say the least.

Cattle had been killed by a grizzly bear around the area and Frank and a young friend were going to be heros and go after the killer bear. Frank had a .44 Henry rifle and his younger friend Lewis McCulley carried a cap and ball pistol.

The young men tracked the bear up near an orchard in the foothills of Cedar Pass by the stage stop and sawmill of Mr. Stough. They had tracked the bear all day and by late evening they made camp near the orchard.

The next morning Frank went out with his axe to cut some firewood. The bear came out of the brush to attack the young man. Frank, armed only with the axe swung it at the bear, only wounding the animal and making him mad and ferocious. The bear retreated, but foolishly Frank went into the brush after him. The bear attacked and severely mauled the young hunter. Lewis heard his friend's screams and ran to help his partner. Armed with only the cap and ball pistol, he shot the bear with all the ammunition he carried. The bear finally ran off leaving the critical wounded Hill heaped in the brush.

The nearest Doctor was in Reno and it was evident that Hill could not make the trip so McCulley took him to the Stough home at the sawmill.

Hill sustained many wounds, the most severe went clear through him from the front of his chest through his back. The wound was filled with dirt, sticks and debris. The best way the men knew to clean it was to thread a silk scarf soaked in whiskey through the wound and pull it back and forth to clean the wound the best they could. One of the men at the mill had a violin and they took the catgut strings from the instrument and soaking them in whiskey to soften and sterilize them they proceeded to sew the suffering man's wounds up.

Frank was too ill to be moved and was expected to die at any moment so they just left him at the mill for the summer. The young bear fighter finally recovered and married and lived to tell the story to his grandchildren. Hill was severely scarred from the incident and the belt he was wearing with the bear teeth holes in it was kept as a reminder of that fearful day.

Hill was happy to know that some Indians had tracked the bear down and killed him after it had attacked him.

Dan Hill married one of the Dodson girls and started their family. Their children were Fred, Elmer, Ray, Ed, Everett, Bertie, Hattie, Mary and Myrtle.

The hard winter of 1889-90 put a lot of people out of business as their stock starved to death. No one had hay to see them through, but Dan Hill had some foresight and had bought hay for $8.00 a ton from Mr. Wade. Mr. Cressler made fun of Hill for paying such a price for hay, and ridiculed him for it. But when the winter was over Hill had his livestock still alive and Cressler was one of the unlucky ones that lost most of his. Many of the stockmen were wiped out.

In 1904 Elmer married Beulah York from Missouri. She came to Cedarville as a young girl and was working in the hotel there when she was sixteen and met the young Elmer Hill.

Elmer and Beulah moved out to a homestead at Mosquito, thirty-eight miles east of Cedarville and in to Nevada at the north end of Long Valley. There, Elmer bought the relinquished homestead from the first homesteader in that valley, Henry Spangler. This was a 320 acre homestead. Beulah took up a Desert Claim which was another 320 acres, which made them a nice spread of 640 acres. Many homesteads has been added to the ranch and it grew to 2500 acres.

Elmer and Beulah's family consisted of four children, Ruby, born 1906, Ervin, born 1907, Opal, born, 1908 and Lucille born 1918.

Ervin was born in Cedarville, but went out to the Mosquito Ranch when he was two years old. He has fond memories of his life out there. But some terrifying ones also. His mother was the post mistress there and the post office was named Beulah. The post offices were named usually for the people that ran them. The closest post office to the south of them was at Vya, Nevada, named after that post mistress, Vya Wimer, (the first girl to be born in Long Valley).

Some of the families in Long Valley, were: Hill, Woods, Diesners, McVickers, Floors, Glass, Coffee, and Fox. At one time there were thirteen kids in the one room school house.

Times were hard and many of the people starved out and moved away. The Hill family had to bring a teacher in to live with them to teach their children as there were was not enough children to have a public school.

When Ervin was thirteen years old he tells of a February day when the school teacher took the four kids for a walk away from the ranch. The school room was in the bunk house attached to the house and it had a bedroom upstairs where a hired man could sleep. Ervin's parents had gone to the Jones place to pump water for the cattle. As the kids walked along the teacher kept stopping and looking back towards the ranch. It was a warm day and the children did not even have their coats or caps on. Finally as they looked back smoke was coming from the house. The children could tell that their home was on fire and went running back. The fire was coming from the upstairs room of the bunk house over the school room. They grabbed buckets of water from the spring and Ervin crawled up a ladder to throw the water into the room where the bed was burning. It looked like someone had left a candle burning to start the bed on fire.

When they looked around, the teacher was looking into the kitchen window where the black smoke was boiling out. She had taken the coal oil lamps from the shelf in the kitchen where Beulah kept them and smashed them on the floor and threw a match into the coal oil and started another fire there.

Nothing could be done now to save anything as the fire was raging so hot. Ruby had crawled into a window at the back of the house into her bedroom and got her typewriter that a railroad man have given her. That was the only item saved from the house. No one even had a coat to get them through the cold wet weather.

Miss Crawford was the teachers name and they found out that she was a firebug, but too late to do them any good. At one time when the family was going to a dance, they had car trouble and turned around and came home. Miss Crawford said she didn't feel good and did not want to go. As the family drove in, they surprised Miss Crawford who was heading to the barn with a lantern, probably to burn the barn that night.

After the fire, Beulah would not live out at Mosquito any longer so the family moved to Cedarville. The teacher just slipped away and nothing was ever done to her.

After the fire, the Beulah Post Office no longer existed and the Post Office was moved over to Diesner and was there from 1920 to 1930. A Blackfoot Indian named Oak Wood ran the mail on horseback.

In 1924 Ervin's Dad traded the Mosquito ranch off and started working on the Big Sage reservoir. He traded the ranch for a place in Escalon, Calif. and moved the family there where Ervin graduated from High School. This is where Ervin started in construction work and started driving truck.

In 1934 Ervin married Mary McCullum and they came back to Cedarville to raise their family, Ernie, Dan, Donnie and Dodie.

The depression hit and the Mosquito ranch was back in the hands of the Hill family. The ranch was defaulted on three times and returned to the Hill's each time. The last time was 1946.

In 1955 Beulah and Elmer bought the Cressler home in Cedarville and moved there.

Ervin can remember the terror that was in everyone's hearts and minds when he was four years old. In 1911 his uncle Fred was a member of the posse that was sent from Surprise Valley on the trail of some renegade Indians. Ervin can remember that Shoshone Mike was a cold blooded son-of-a-gun that terrorized all that came in his path.

Indian problems prevailed in the Modoc Country in the late 1800's and early 1900's. The last massacre in the north country of that eastern corner of California took place in 1911. It started on the California side but they trailed across into Nevada in Little High Rock Canyon.

The turn of events left four men dead after a freshly butchered steer was found. A sheep herder, Bertrand Indiano had no weapon with him when he had left the sheep camp of Humphrey-Cambron Cattle Co. that January morning in 1911.

The young sheepherder was out looking for lost sheep when he came upon blood stains in the snow. Upon further investigation he found a freshly butchered steer. He suspected someone needed meat for their family and was not too alarmed. It could possible have been rustlers. He decided to return to the camp with the news of his find.

Indiano made his way slowly down the canyon with a spooky feeling that he was being watched.

Back at the ranch Harry Cambron, the owner and two other sheep herders, John Laxague and Peter Erramouspe were waiting. When the story of the butchered steer was told, it was decided to investigate further.

The next morning the party of four men headed out. Only Cambron carried a weapon, a single revolver. The men came upon the dead animal and started to dismount when war cries of several Indians pierced the air. The three sheepherders, Laxague, Erramouspe, and Indiano were killed

Mosquito Ranch, the Hills' homestead.

Reuben Albaugh and Elmer Hill, Mosquito Ranch, Nevada.

immediately, but Cambron managed to get one shot off killing one Indian before he was killed.

When Indiano first found the butchered steer, the Indians could have killed him, but they were laying a trap and it worked.

Ervin's father had gone to town to get medicine for one of the sick children, leaving his mother and the children at the ranch. "If those renegade Indians had come over our way I wouldn't be here telling you this story," he declared.

It could be weeks before anyone would miss the four men as it was a huge vast country and no communication. Not hearing from anyone for three weeks, a cowboy, Warren Fruits and a Mr. Bryant decided to ride up to the line camp. They found no one in camp and it looked like it had been deserted for some time. The two men rode on up the canyon, and by chance and much to their horror they rode up on the scene of the massacre. They found the bodies of the four men in a willow thicket piled in a heap and partially covered with snow.

Fruits and Bryant headed back to the nearest ranch, the sheep camp operated by Humphrey-Cambron Company and found Charles Demick, area manager for Miller and Lux and Sid Street an Eagleville rancher.

All four men rode on to Eagleville across the California border to report the disaster. A posse was sent out to retrieve the bodies.

Ervin Hill at Diesner, Nevada.

Another posse was immediately formed of twenty-two men with Demick in charge, and on February 16, 1911 four weeks after the murders, the posse left Eagleville.

The posse consisted of Lawmen, sheepmen, cattle ranchers and citizens of that area of California and Nevada. Sheriff Elzie Smith of Modoc County; Fred Hill, (Ervin's uncle); Henry Hughs; William Parsons; Ed Hogle; George Holmes; Joe Reeder; Jack Ferguson; Ben Cambron (brother of one of the victims); Warren Fruits; Mort West; Frank Perry; O.D. Van Norman; Sid Street; Gilbert Jackson; James Baty; Sheriff Ferril, Washoe County, Nevada; Captain Donnelly of Nevada State Police and three of his men Neward, Stone and Duck.

At first Indians were not suspected as the Paiutes had been peaceable for years and none were known to be in the area. At first it was thought that a band of rustlers were guilty.

When the Posse arrived they found items that made them believe it was Indians. The remains of a brush wickiup (dwelling) was the deciding factor that Indians were to blame.

The trail was plain to follow in the frozen snow, but the Indians soon split up with the women and children going one direction and the braves the other. The posse split to follow the trails, but the trails later crossed and the Indians camped together at night. The next day the Indians fanned out and went in every direction making tracking almost impossible.

All the ammunition of the posse was packed on one mule and the animal was guarded carefully so the Indians could not spook him off. This seemed to be an idiotic plan for all the ammunition to be in one place rather than split among the men.

Finally the posse tracked the Indians to Paradise Valley thirty miles North of Winnemucca. Some men had to leave the posse as their horses had given out on them. The weary men went on to Golconda where they set up headquarters. Scouts were sent out to look for signs of the Indians. They finally found the renegades camped at Kelly Creek.

On February 25 nine days and two hundred miles later the posse could see campfire smoke and see the tethered horses.

The posse attempted to sneak up on the Indians but were spotted by a squaw that went screaming back to camp.

The battle was on with guns blazing. The Indian Scout with the Posse, Skinny Pascal, was sent to tell the Indians to surrender. He approached the Indians and quickly returned to report, "Boys they no quit, shoot quick".

Shots were exchanged and three Indians were killed, one being Shoshone Mike, the renegade Apache.

Captain Donnelly shouted not to shoot the woman and children. He shouted it so loudly that the squaws heard him and stood before their men to protect them from the gun fire from the posse. Ed Hogle was shot and killed. It was later learned that the bullet that killed Hogle was the last bullet the Indians had.

O.D. VanNorman and George Holmes captured a fifteen year old squaw. They said she fought like a wild tiger but after she calmed down, she gave the account of what had happened during the massacre and the pursuit of the Indians.

When the Indians had left the reservation they had raided a Miller and Lux ranch and killed the Chinese cook and stole some horses. When they saw Indiano in Little High Rock Canyon they thought he was a law officer and then when he returned with the other three men they were sure of it so they ambushed the foursome and massacred them. Thus the beginning and end of the last Indian War in the West.

Glorianne Weigand
October 2, 1995.

The Wimer homestead at Vya, Nevada.

Arlo the Lumberjack

Mother began crying, she had finally recognized me. Young Lewis Eades sat at the dinner table with a family he had not seen for five years, his family.

During the civil war it was not uncommon for a wealthy family to pay a young man to go to the battle field in place of their own beloved son. This is what had happened to young Lewis Eades, the son of Granville and Rosanna Eades. Young Lewis was born in Monroe County Indiana in 1846. His brothers Granville Jr., Isom and Andrew had traveled with their parents in a wagon train from St. Joseph, Missouri with the Sylvester and Turnbull families to Oregon where Mr. Eades ran a sawmill near Lebanon. He soon left that mill and moved on to northern California in Modoc County and settled near Egg Lake for a short time. The Eades family then moved to the town of Dana and started another mill. At Egg Lake Granville told of grass as high as a horses back, and the geese and ducks so plentiful that there cackling made such a noise that you could not carry on a conversation with the man standing next to you.

Granville Eades had come from Kentucky where he was born in 1822. He had married Rosanna Shyes from New York. Their first son Lewis was born in 1846 in Monroe County, Indiana, Granville Jr. 1849, Isom was born in 1850, Andrew in 1852, Rebecca Jane 1854, William 1856, George 1857, Thomas 1859, Calvin 1861, Amanda 1863, Jake 1865 and Ada 1865. Most of the children were born in Kentucky, Indiana and Iowa before the family traveled west.

When the Eades family left for California, young Lewis was left at the mercy of the soldiers of the Civil War. The North fighting against the South. Stories are told that the young soldiers received fifty dollars in gold to join the service, and young Eades had received the money from the wealthy family to go in place of their own son. The young soldier, Lewis was only fifteen years old when his family left and went west to get away from the raging battles. Lewis soon had all of the fighting he could take and ran away.

Lewis and a young friend headed west, where Lewis had heard his family had moved to several years before. The two young men traveled together horse back until they came to the great Salt Lake. Lewis' young friend had gone as far as he wanted and he turned back. The young Eades traveled on alone asking the friendly Indians along the way to direct him to California. They pointed to the West and told Lewis to follow the sitting sun. After a long lonely trip the young Eades trail led him to Susanville, California. There he was directed to keep traveling and he crossed the Hat Creek rim. He was told to travel on following the large stream until he came to a water falls and he would be getting near Dana where his family lived. He traveled until he came to what is now known as Burney Falls and went on to the Eades family homestead at Dana.

Young Lewis knocked on the door and his father Granville answered his knock. He knew at once his father did not recognize him. He had grown a lot in those five long years and had a full beard on his face. The young man asked if Mr. Eades might be in need of some help, as he was looking for a job. Lewis was invited in to the home and offered a meal. Part way through the meal, Rosanna began crying, she recognized her son that she had not seen for so long. She had not known if he was dead or alive.

Lewis stayed at Dana for awhile then moved over the hill to Gouger Neck in Modoc County. Lewis visited the Carmichael Mill at Taylor Creek at the edge of Big Valley and soon married a daughter of Moses Carmichael, Calista. Her sister Sarah had married William Gerig.

When Lewis first came to Lookout in 1869 there was only a trading post. Lewis traveled on a few miles north where he built a log cabin at Gouger Neck. It later burned down.

Lewis and Calista's family consisted of Agnes, Raymond, Arch, Doris, Maude, Ina, Julie, and Jenny. Lewis raised cattle and was a rancher. Their homestead is now what is known as the Landes ranch along Pit River. Calista died at an early age from complications of an abscessed tooth.

Lewis' brother Isom was one of the three men accused and acquitted of the Lookout Lynching in 1901. All the men in Lookout were taken to Alturas for the trial. The women and children were left in Lookout. The Indians were restless and riled up. They worried the women as they circled the town constantly on their horses. The apprehensive women spent the nights in the Trowbridge store where there was one man to stand guard over them. The towns men were held in Alturas for months.

Isom had a family, his wife was an Indian woman that had run away from the camp of the renegade Indian Captain Jack at the Lava Beds. The young woman came to the home of Isom with her young son Jeff and

Isom took them in. Jeff was very young and Eades adopted him. Jeff Eades turned out to be quite a cowboy and worked on many ranches in the area including Dixie Valley. He was well thought of. Isom and his wife had two daughters. Isom had been a wealthy rancher with a big herd of cattle, but it took most of his money to fight his battle to prove his innocence in the hanging. This also broke his spirit and he died a few years later. His wife and daughters went back to the Klamath Indian Reservation in Oregon.

The Potter family was another pioneer family that came to the Egg Lake country. This family were lumber men. John Potter and his partner Charlie Gooch started a mill at Egg Lake. John had married Minnie Adams and they had quite a family. Gertrude (Gertie), Marie, Amy, Dick, Bessie, Lowell, Velt, Forest, Joe, Jim, and Faye.

Gooch moved on to Little Hot Springs Valley near the town of Day. John Potter was known for the unique wedding gift that he would give to each young married couple. He would cut the finest board from the heart of a log, twenty-four inches by two inches by sixteen feet long, a premium board for the young couple to use for a drain board in their new homes.

The Potter children would move to Lookout in the winter time with their mother so they could go to school. The school house was on the East side of the river. Little Gertie Potter could remember the day the men were hung from the bridge as they would not let her and her sister cross the bridge to go to school and they had to turn around and go home.

Arch Eades took Gertie Potter as his bride in 1914. The young couple drove their team and buggy to the county seat of Alturas which was a two day trip. They were married there and stayed in the Niles Hotel before making the return trip. Gertie was 20 years old and Arch was 30 years old. They moved back to their home in Gouger Neck next to the Shaw ranch. A son was born and died in infancy. In 1918 Arlo was born and the family moved to Lookout. Amie was born in 1919, Hope in 1922 and Fern in 1927. All the births were attended by mid-wife Mrs. Leventon.

Arch Eades was quite a cowboy and worked around Likely where he broke calvary horses for the army. Arch and Gertie milked twenty cows and had quite a herd of beef cattle. Arch was the road foreman for the building of the road from Lookout to Adin.

Gertie could tell of the dances that were held every Saturday night. She certainly loved to dance. They would travel for hours to go to a dance and have a big potluck midnight supper. They would dance until daylight then eat breakfast before traveling home.

The days of prohibition was really a sore spot with Gertie, she said it was the ruination of the country. She could remember the bootleggers with their stills in the mountains around Lookout. She told of the old

Minnie and John Potter, 1893.

Arch and Gertie Eades, 1914.

Model A cars that had the gas tanks filled with bootleg whiskey and how they would stop at each culvert along the road to fill the jugs left by people that wanted a little moonshine. The car would have a gallon gas can full to run on while the gas tank was filled with the illegal whiskey. The women started drinking and the young boys would steal the illegal booze and sell it, getting themselves in trouble.

A lot of epidemics of flu and diphtheria ravaged the country. There were no Doctors at Lookout and it was a long way horseback to get a doctor from Adin or Lookout. Some families would lose several children at a time with the dreaded diseases.

John Potter moved his mill from Egg Lake closer to Lookout. The first mill was built in 1906 then in 1924 it was moved eight miles west of Lookout. The logs were brought to the mill by teams of horses and the mill was run by steam boilers. Minnie Potter cooked for twelve men at the cook house at the mill and also cared for her large brood of children. The Potter Mill ran for sixty years.

John Potter went in debt for $2,200.00 for a steam engine for the mill and at the time he felt that this was as much as the national debt. Mr. Potter fell from a lumber pile and landed on his head. He was taken to Susanville to the hospital but never regained consciousness and died a few days later. He was around seventy years old. After their fathers death, Joe, Jim, Forest and Dick Potter ran the mill for several years.

Arch and Gertie Eades went on with their family. Their son Arlo started to school in Lookout and when recess came, he walked home thinking the school day had ended. The Eades family had moved to a ranch just south of Lookout and Arch ranched there. Arlo can remember the boys in the eighth grade were so big and were shaving. Some of them were eighteen and twenty years old. Mrs. Francis Summers was the teacher that they heckled so bad.

In 1933 when the Lookout fire erupted in the Leventon barn, Arlo can remember he and Hugh Stevens were swimming in the river. They ran to help and several teenage boys carried a large piano out of one of the homes. They were so excited and carried it without much trouble, but after the fire it was so heavy they could barely budge it. The fire devastated Lookout burning many homes and businesses.

The winters were hard and cold and lots of snow. The winter of 1934-35 there was so much snow the mail stage had not been able to get through from Bieber for quite some time. Herb Hayes was taking the important mail through on horseback. There were no road graders to plow the roads. The men from Lookout took their shovels and started shoveling out the road, and the men from Bieber took their shovels and started shoveling from their end. Several days and many aching backs later the six miles of road had been opened so the mail could get through.

Arlo took his first job for Cox and Clarke at the Dixie Valley ranch when he was sixteen. He thought he was quite a cowboy. He and Durwood Oiler went there together to help on the hay crew. It was quite a busy place and Arlo can remember the huge ten or twelve big hay stacks. Arlo worked with the horses driving buck rake and was always ready for the good meals served in the large dining room. There were about forty men to be fed by the cook. Besides the cook there was a baker, dishwasher and chore boy to milk the cows and keep the firewood box filled. Some of the men took turns going out after firewood. One day after they had loaded the load of wood out in the hills and were heading home, the team ran away. There were no brakes on the wagon and they were going down hill. Iverson Barnes was pinned beneath the wagon and broke his hip. One of the horses was killed. It was quite a wreck.

Arlo went back to high school at Adin where he met his sweetheart and he and Kittie Wright were married in 1938. Kittie had come from Colorado with her parents. Her father Scotty Wright logged for the Edgerton Lumber Company of Adin. Kittie and Arlo had three sons

Eades family: Arlo, Buzzy, Gary, Lennie and Kittie, 1944.

Buzzy, Gary and Lennie. Arlo's sisters married, Amy married Stanford Thayer and had three children, Smiley, Rosalie and Ben. Hope married Howard Yeager and had four sons Bob, Buck, Dan and Matt. Fern married Andy Morse and had three daughters, Nancy, Karen and Susan.

Arlo went into the Army in 1944 and served in the Philippine Islands. This was an active two years in his life and one he will always remember. Arlo was sick with malaria while in the service. When his tour of duty was about over he was sent back to his homeland on the ship where he served as cooks helper. They were on the ship for the holidays and at Thanksgiving, Arlo helped cook two hundred turkeys for the troops.

Arlo returned to his country and his family. With his cowboy life and army life behind him he started what would be his lifelong occupation and his true love of work. The first job after the service was working at the sawmill in Burney. He then went to work at Round Mountain at the Zamboni mill. After breaking his arm two times he decided to move back to Lookout where Arlo started working in the timber and started falling trees. This only seemed to be a natural occupation for him as his Great Grandfather Carmichael owned a sawmill, his grandfather Eades and Potter both owned sawmills. Sawdust was in his blood.

Arlo and Kittie moved to Lookout and Arlo started out falling timber for the McCloud River Lumber Company at Whitehorse. Fallers were being paid forty-nine cents a board foot. You also received $5.00 a day show up time and if you worked really hard you could make $20.00 a day.

Arlo had many different partners and they used a two man hand saw. Timber falling was hard back breaking work, but it paid the best wage. Weekends the men from the lumber camps went home to their families. There were quite a few family homes at Whitehorse. They had the cook house, bunk houses, Union Hall, railroad depot, store, school and a farm where they raised their own hogs. Crum Meat Co. would come get the live hogs and take them to butcher so the cook house would have fresh hams and bacon for the crew. You paid eighty cents for each meal. The men ate breakfast and supper at the cookhouse and took a brown bag lunch for noon. Weekends, Thanksgiving and Christmas were the only days you had off. Arlo lived at Whitehorse in the bunkhouse where he got his bed, blankets and laundry done. There were about sixty men fed at the cookhouse where there was a cook, baker, dishwasher and lunch maker.

In 1950 the gas chain saw was invented and this was a marvelous machine for the timber faller. The lumber company furnished the saw for fallers. The large two man saws with a fifty inch blade weighed about seventy pounds. They cost around $300.00 for the first ones Arlo can remember.

McCloud Lumber company had a lot of caterpillars. The railroad built spurs to get closer to the timber that was being fallen. They would drag the thirty-two foot logs up to a quarter of a mile, and sometimes dragging four to five logs at a time. The rigging crew would hook up the logs then drag them to the rail road flat cars where they were loaded by steam jammers. The logs were then sent to McCloud to be sawed into lumber. The McCloud mill could cut one hundred million board feet per year.

After the White Horse camp was closed down, the houses were loaded on to the flat cars and moved on to the next camp at Widow Valley. When the timber was harvested there, the houses were then loaded on the flat cars again and moved to Camp Kinyon at Pondosa.

The camps were moved to the trees in the area of the railroad instead of hauling the logs for miles by truck as is the practice today. The homes were also moved on flat cars as that was the day before mobile homes.

When Arlo worked at Pondosa and Camp Kinyon the family moved there. Kittie was the post master at that camp. Arlo worked out of the Pondosa camp for sixteen years.

While Arlo was falling timber near Bartle he and his partner cut the biggest tree he can remember. The giant Doug Fir tree measured ten feet in diameter. The men fell the tree with a power saw with a fifty inch blade. When they finally got it on the ground, the caterpillar had to keep

Arlo cutting big tree.

rolling it so he could cut through it.

The big tree was cut into around twenty logs. The first three or four logs had to be cut in only sixteen foot lengths because it was so big. The top of the gigantic tree was called a school marm with five forks that were large enough to be cut into individual logs. As the tree fell, some of the forks broke and had to be cut into shorter lengths of ten or twelve feet. It was an all day job to just cut up the one tree. It scaled over 20,000 board feet.

The winter of 1952 was one of the blue snow that Paul Bunyan could relate to. Arlo was falling timber at Bartle on top of Dead Horse Mountain. There was eight foot of snow. Each pair of timber fallers had a two man shovel crew to work ahead of them. The shovel crew would shovel four feet down around the tree to be cut, making steps into the bank for the fallers. The fallers would crawl down into the hole and cut the trees then duck down into the hole as the tree fell onto the deep snow. Still today you can see the four and five foot stumps at Dead Horse Summit left as a reminder of the deep snow.

After falling timber for twenty years at Whitehorse, Pondosa and Bartle, Arlo started scaling the logs. Scaling is a term used for measuring the logs to determine the board feet that they contained. Scaling is a very important job so the owners of the timber would be paid for the lumber that was cut from their logs. Arlo really enjoyed this job and was soon promoted to check scaler. At this job he did a lot of traveling checking the scalers that were under him. He check scaled for P.G.&E. and Southern Pacific. His area included from Klamath Falls, Oregon, to Quincy, Mt. Shasta, and Redding in California and all points in between. The counties of Siskiyou, Modoc, Lassen, Plumas and Truckee were his area. Arlo scaled and check scaled for a total of twenty years, totaling forty years that he worked in the lumber industry. He really loved his job and enjoyed meeting people. This was the happiest time of his life. Arlo thought he would try retirement and has retired three times, but as his daughter-in-law Edna tells it, he loves to work more than any man she ever saw.

The Eades family is still carrying on with the fifth generation in the lumber business. Arlo and Kittie's son Buzzy is a Forester for Kimberly Clark and was delegated to talk to President Clinton on the spotted owl issue. He owns Eades Timber Resources. Buzzy married Muriel Crum and they have four children. Their son is in the timber industry. Lennie and his cousin Delbert Gould are partners in E & G Logging. Lennie married Edna Methvin and they have two children. Gary and his wife Mary Jo had four children. Gary is deceased.

Even though Arlo may have taught his sons a lot of what they know about the timber business, he said he never worked for them as he never wanted them to be his boss.

Today Arlo is still working for Modoc County at the Adin transfer station where he can meet with people and visit with them. He rolls with the punches and gets along with everyone. He said if a Democrat comes in, he is a Democrat and if a Republican comes in he is a Republican. It works better that way and he makes it a policy not to talk politics.

At the age of 77 Arlo is still going strong. His mother Gertie lived to be 97 years of age so he has another twenty years at least to delight all who meet him, because he is not ready to retire for the fourth time yet.

Glorianne Weigand
November 5, 1995

Fred Hansen and Arlo Eades in 1952 at Bartle—tree was 8'2" in diameter.

Albert on one of his prize pumpkins.

The Bar Double H Ranch

WANTED!
YANKEE POT ROAST
AND WILD RICE PADDY
REWARD YOUR APPETITE TODAY!
EAT MORE BEEF

This is the sign painted on the wooden white washed barn at the Albaugh ranch along the Pittville road and seen by all that pass by. This is the barn where Albert Albaugh started his career of milking cows seventy years ago and where his love of ranching all started. Born and bred to be a rancher in 1917 and still loving every minute of it. Even though Albert and Elizabeth Albaugh retired several years ago they still live on the ranch and Albert has his chickens and milked a cow until just recently when his old milk cow died.

One of Alberts' earliest memories was of the InterMountain Fair when he was four years old. He was so anxious to go to the fair, until he saw what his mother had for him to wear. His mother Minnie had a new little brown suit made for Albert with short pants and long stockings. He hated that suit, he did not want to wear it, but his choice was to wear the suit or not go to the fair. Much to his displeasure he wore the suit, but still thinks of it today.

That was the earliest Fair that Albert can remember, but it is doubtful that he has missed many since then. Albert has been a much loved and respected member of the InterMountain Fair board for eighteen years. Albert with his smiling face and sunny disposition is in attendance at each and every fair and most of the functions in the McArthur area. Especially at all the high school football and basketball games.

Albert, the youngest of six children of William John Albaugh and Minnie Baker Albaugh still lives on the home ranch where he was born and his roots run deep in the fertile soil along the Pit River.

The Albaughs,
Back: Anna,
Reuben, Willis.
Front: Velma,
Minnie, Albert,
W.J. and Ed.

154

W.J. Albaugh, called Billie by his wife was born in 1867 in Pennsylvania and at the age of seventeen he was tired of picking up rocks on the ranch. He talked of going to work on the railroad, but his Mother said she would rather see him go west. W.J. had heard exciting accounts of the Indian wars and the buffalo hunting and thought this would be an exciting life for him.

With thirty dollars in his pocket he bought a train ticket for as far as his money would take him. It took $28.80 to buy a ticket to Kansas, so that was his destination. Landing there he got a job sprouting potatoes. Boarding the train again he rode west in a stock car with six stallion horses. Hiding in the hay when the brakeman would pass through the car. There was only suppose to be one hired hand riding with the horses and W.J. didn't want to get caught. After landing in Weiser, Idaho, and paying for his breakfast he had a quarter in his pocket. W.J. got a shave and bought a cigar then went to work again sprouting potatoes.

A ruckus broke out in Weiser and he saw a friend of his shot so he thought it was a good time to move on to Portland, Oregon where he got a job clearing some brush with some chinamen. One of the chinamen laid his shovel down and young Albaugh thought it was better than his and thought the Chinaman was done with it so he picked it up to use it. This was not the thing to do and W.J. soon learned of his mistake and decided it was time to move on. Next the young man moved on to McCloud, California to become a logger.

Cutting and selling wood for $3.00 a cord which made him $1.50 a cord profit was young Albaughs next occupation.

In 1893 the banks went broke. Albaugh had a little cash and he loaned $10.00 to a friend, taking his watch for pay.

W.J. decided to try his hand at gold mining. He cut shakes to trade for a grub stake, but decided to trade some of the grub back for a frying pan. Redding, California was the nearest town which was just a little town with a couple of paved streets. Mining was hard and working as hard as he could he never made more than twenty-five cents a day.

The young Albaugh heard there were jobs feeding cows in the Fall River Valley and headed north east. Arriving there with only a pack on his back, he made that his home for the rest of his life. The young man slept in barns and worked on ranches.

It was 1894 and ten years after the young pioneer had left his home and his parents. Stopping by the Baker ranch he was asked to stay for supper. This is where he met his future bride, Wilhelmina (Minnie) Baker. In 1896 W.J. Albaugh and Minnie Baker were married. The young newlyweds moved to the Shaw place and started raising their family. Willis was born in 1898, Anna in 1899 and Reuben in 1901.

In 1902 Minnie told her husband to go buy back her parents' homestead. They bought the home ranch back from the Oliver family in 1902 for $2700.00. After moving to their new home their other three children were born, Ed in 1909, Velma in 1912 and Albert in 1917. Willis was nearly twenty years older than Albert, so Albert truly was the baby of the family.

Minnie Baker was born in 1876 near Red Bluff, Calif. and the youngest of six children. Her father Reuben Baker was a rancher and freighter. The family came to the Fall River Valley when Minnie was six years old in 1882, settling on the present Albaugh ranch, Minnie had to quit school when she was in the sixth grade when her mother died. Minnie became the woman of the home and took over the duties of her mother.

The patent rights to the homestead were issued to Steve Hollenbeak December, 1878 for 160 acres. July 1879 it was deeded to Daniel Tarter for $1,600. September 1880 it was deeded to William Fullerton for $2,100. June 1885 deeded to Reuben Baker for $2,000. Baker mortgaged to Oliver in 1888 for $2,500, Oliver died in 1890 and the place was sold at public auction for $4,650.35 to Ellen Oliver, administrator. The ranch was rented out for several years to McCoy, Blake and Raudy, then in 1902 William J. and Minnie Albaugh bought it for $2,700 from George Oliver.

W.J. Albaugh was a well known and prominent cattleman of the Fall River Valley. When people would ask him what was his success story, he said he had something to sell every day. He had a small dairy, sheep, hogs, chickens and cattle. He sold milk, cream, butter, eggs, apples and wood.

From 1902 until 1920 the Albaugh's Bar Double H ranch was a very popular place. It was used for a stopping point for cattle drives to the rail heads in Bartle and Redding. At times there would be 2,000 cattle assembled on this ranch where they were weighed, fed, and sorted for market. The cowboys were fed and boarded at the Albaugh home. Many old time cattle buyers such as Pete Huff, Al Conner, Billie Woods and Bill Paulk stayed at the Albaugh ranch. The cattle drives stopped when the railroad was completed in Nubieber in 1930.

In 1908 W.J. acquired grazing rights in Modoc County in the McAfee Flat, Egg Lake Country from the Red River Lumber Company and U.S. Forest Service. At one time they had a permit for four hundred head and a cow and her calf could graze for $2.50 per unit for a five month grazing period. In early years two and three year old steers were sold.

In 1909 W.J. built a new two story home for his growing family. A hard worker himself, he taught his children to be hard workers. He would not tolerate a lazy person or a complainer. He ruled with an iron hand.

A favorite one of his sayings was if you could not be on time to an appointment, be ten minutes early, and he lived by this rule. W.J. had a saying that when things get tough, that's the time to hold on because the other fellow is about to let go and when he does things will get better for you.

When Albert was four years old his older brother Reuben who was twenty years old came and took Albert by the hand. He said he had something to give the little boy. Walking hand in hand down to the barn Reuben presented Albert with a new born pinto colt. It was to be his very own. Albert soon named the colt "Pinto", and proudly rode the horse all the years to grammar school and to high school. He loved that horse and all the kids in the family would ride him. At one time they took a picture of thirteen kids on him. Pinto lived to be twenty-five years old.

While riding him to grammar school at Pittville, Albert would chase the girls on Pinto. The girls would run screaming up on the porch and Albert would ride his horse right up on the porch after them, and the girls would run into the school house.

The teachers Albert had at Pittville were Nellie Callison, Bessie Wilcox, Ruby Bosworth and Frances Gassaway. His sister Velma was in the eighth grade when he was in the first, so he didn't go to school with his brothers and sisters.

One time Marvin Hollenbeak was mad and slammed a book down on the desk. The teacher Bessie Wilcox was a pretty stout woman and she picked Marvin up and slammed him up and down like he did the book. Albert was thinking out loud and said, "bet you can't do that to me", the teacher heard him and grabbed him. Albert was holding on to the seat of his desk as hard as he could and the teacher pulled him so hard the screws that held the seat to the floor came loose, and Albert, seat and all came up. Albert was taken to the front of the room and the yard stick was used on him. That sure cured him of thinking out loud.

Albert went on to McArthur to high school and this is where he met Elizabeth Doty, the girl that he would later take as his bride.

Elizabeth was from a prominent ranching family from the Hat Creek area. Her mother Iva Morris was born in 1882 at Coos Bay, Oregon. Her parents Horace and Annie Morris had come from Missouri in 1873 after they were married. Horace came west to Nevada and worked on a ranch learning to raise alfalfa. Moving around quite a bit they arrived by boat at Coos Bay. When they decided to travel back to northern California they drove two wagons. Annie drove one and Horace drove one. There were five children, William, Ernest, Walker, Ada and Iva. Mrs. Morris drove a wagon all day, set up camp at night and cooked for a family of seven. She never wanted to re-live the "GOOD OLE DAYS".

Settling finally near Whitmore, California, Horace peddled beans, dried fruit and any commodity that was saleable. He peddled from Fall River valley through Modoc County and through Fandango Pass by wagon. He also freighted from Redding to the stores in the Fall River valley.

In 1889 the Morris family bought a place on Hat Creek and moved there. Local Indians were hired to help clear the land of timber, rocks and brush. A small patch of hay was planted with each clearing. When it was time to harvest it, it was cut by hand with a scythe and hand raked and pitched onto the wagons. Horace was the first person on Hat Creek to raise alfalfa. The land was never plowed, just harrowed with a hand made harrow then the seed was sown. The Morris family had quite a few milk cows and started a few beef cows. They raised geese to harvest the down for pillows and mattresses. When it was time to harvest the down a sock was pulled over the head of the goose and the down was plucked from the bird. During the summer they could harvest the down about three times.

There was no school at Hat Creek, so the older brother William moved to Fall River so he could go to school. The younger children went by horse and buggy eight miles to school at Cassel. The Lincoln school at Hat Creek was built in 1898 and the children only had a mile to walk to school.

In 1903 Iva went to Chico normal school to become a teacher and she graduated in 1908. The young teacher had various teaching jobs, one being at Goose Valley, several miles away and she rode her horse to her teaching job.

While teaching at Anderson, Calif. she was appointed Shasta County "Girls County Canning Club Leader". In 1914 the "County Canning Club was dropped and the County 4-H Clubs" were established.

In 1910 a twenty-three year old man from New York, Asa Doty, arrived by train at Sisson, California, (now known as Mt. Shasta). There was three feet of snow and the thermometer registered zero degrees. He traveled by sleigh to Dana, then four horse buckboard stage to Fall River Mills and boarded another stage to Cassel, his final destination.

Asa had come to Cassel to build a creamery and install the equipment. This was his expertise that he had learned in New York at Cornell University. While in Cassel he met the school marm that he would later marry.

On 1914 Asa went to Lookout to run the cheese factories and on to Alturas to build and run that one. Most of the creameries in that corner of California had the hand of Asa Doty in them somewhere.

In 1917 Asa decided to travel to Alaska to see the northern lights. Landing at Skagway he heard of a mining job at Dawson 340 miles away. Heading out for the gold fields, Asa walked to Dawson. There were road houses every eighteen or twenty miles. If you didn't make it to the next road house each night you slept along the trail and had nothing to eat. It was a long hard grueling trip but Asa made it in twelve days. The mining job was slinging an eight pound sledge. The ground had to be thawed by forcing steam through holes to dig for the gold. It was not quite as glamourous of a job as he had thought it would be.

Asa joined the Army and traveled all over the U.S.A., Alaska and Canada by train and boat.

Asa had kept in touch by letters with the school marm from Hat Creek and even though he had only seen her a couple of times he asked her to meet him in Portland, Oregon and in 1919 Asa Doty and Iva Morris were married.

Asa and Iva traveled by a lumber boat to San Francisco then back to Hat Creek where they moved in with Iva's parents as her mother was quite ill. Iva taught at the Lincoln school.

Elizabeth was born in 1921, and her brother Morris was born in 1923. They went to the Lincoln school and when it was time for them to go to high school they went to McArthur.

Asa became quite ill and had to spend a year and a half in the hospital and had a kidney removed. Iva ran the ranch and raised the children. The Doty family raised hay and fed cattle for others to market their hay. They fattened cattle out for the Royce packing plant in Fall River. A lot of cattle were driven to the Doty ranch to be weighed as they were one of the few who had a livestock scale. The cattle were then driven to Bartle to be loaded on the stock cars of the train. In 1925 they bought cattle of their own. In 1937 their home burned and they lost everything they owned.

When Elizabeth went to high school in McArthur she met a young good looking guy who loved to play basketball. Albert Albaugh caught her eye. After school graduation in 1938 Elizabeth went on to college at U.C. Davis for two years and got her first degree in Home Ec. Then went on to Oregon State at Corvallis, Oregon where she graduated. The war was on and the thing to do was join the service. Elizabeth was sent to Arkansas to take the test for administration. She wanted to be in cooks and bakers, so she purposely flunked the typing test. The WACS sent her to run the nurses mess hall at Tilton General Hospital at Ft. Dix, New Jersey.

Graduating from high school in 1936 Albert went on to Davis to college much to the delight of his older brother Reuben that spent his lifetime affiliated with the University of California at Davis. Two years at Davis and Albert took animal husbandry, bee keeping, dairy and sheep production. Albert was also on the wrestling team. He took a non degree course then the lonely country boy went back home to the ranch. It was summer time and during haying and Albert was called to the Army, but he got a deferment to help get the crops in. In the Fall he enlisted into the Air Corp and was sent to North Africa and Egypt where he was in the Military Police.

While in the service Albert was writing to his high school sweetheart Elizabeth Doty. Both of them were due for a furlough, so they decided to get married while they were on leave. They met in Reno and traveled on to Hat Creek to be married at the Doty home. August 14, 1945, V.J. Day they were united in marriage. Albert's sister Anna McArthur loaned them her car to take a honeymoon trip. As it was war time she even gave them her gas rationing stamps. The newlyweds drove the short trip to Lassen Park and rented a cabin. All of a sudden all of the horns started honking and the news had been received that the war was over. What a relief. Both Albert and Elizabeth had to return to their bases to be discharged, but in a few months they had returned to the Albaugh ranch to start their new life together.

Minnie and W.J. Albaugh.

Asa and Iva Doty.

Albert and Elizabeth went into a partnership with his brother Willis and his wife Mary on the Bar Double H Albaugh ranch. Albert bought several hundred cows from his Dad at $90.00 a head.

The Albaugh brothers ran their cows on spring range on the bench along Big Valley mountain then drove them to the Egg Lake Forest Service allotment in June. The cattle would start drifting home in the fall and they were gathered by deer season so the cowboys didn't have to dodge the bullets.

Willis was the camp cook and when he retired Albert had Roy Cessna, Frankie Lee, or Frank Parker to do the cooking for the trail riding crew. Albert never liked to cook, and Elizabeth teases him that he sold the cattle and the range permit in 1965 because he ran out of camp cooks.

Albert's documents of appreciation line a complete wall and are all well deserved. Among them are 1988 Fireman of the Year, 1986 Citizen of the Year, 50 Years Alpha Gamma Rho Fraternity, 40 Years Commissioner of the Fire District, Charter Member of the Inter-Mountain Cattleman and President 1960, 61 and 62, 45 Years Pine Grove Mosquito District, Twenty-five years buyer at the Junior Livestock Auction, Eighteen Years Inter-Mountain Fair Board Member.

Elizabeth is a Charter Member of the American National Cattle-Women and in 1956 she started the Inter-Mountain Cattlewomen of which she is a valuable member.

Albert and Elizabeth have three children. Their daughter Cara Lynn and her husband Virgil Gosser have two daughters, Anna Marie and Amy, son Allen has two children Erin and Jared, and son Stephen and his wife Elena have two children Trina and Clint.

The ranch that Albert bought from his dad in 1946 he sold to his son Stephen in 1980. Things have changed some on the Albaugh ranch, but Stephen and Allen are like their grandfather and believe you should not put all of your eggs in one basket. Most of the cattle have been sold, but some still roam the rolling hills of the ranch. The nineteen year old long horn steer died, but his horns hang above the fireplace in the Albaugh home. The third generation Albaughs now raise mint, wild rice, carrot seed, garlic, hay, sheep and cows. Albert like his sons worked very close

Elizabeth and Albert, 40th anniversary, 1985.

Albert and Ruben in the parade.

with Farm Advisors and the University of California in tests of every kind to better their livestock and crops.

Recently a mountain lion took a toll on their lamb crop and killed eighteen lambs. A few at a time would be killed and buried by the cunning cat. The chickens started missing at night or found dead. Albert suspected a coon or a weasel, so he decided to take a stand and get the culprit. After dark Albert seated himself on a bucket in the chicken house and armed with his 410 shot gun. In the dark he saw something move, ka-boom, echoed from the chicken house, and the black barn cat lay dead. Albert went back to the house feeling a little guilty, and the next morning the dead cat was missing. The mountain lion came by and packed it off. The lion could have been looking right down Albert's shirt collar. In a few days traps were set and the lion was trapped in the chicken house.

An exciting event in Albert and Elizabeth's life was Sept. 6, 1991. Nine-thirty in the evening Elizabeth was in bed and Albert had just gotten out of the shower when the loudest noise you could imagine was heard. The wind had really started kicking up and a huge pine tree that stood by the house fell on the house. The sparks were flying when it hit the power line, but the Albaughs thought the house had been hit by lightning. Albert standing only in his bath towel was only missed by inches where the tree fell across the bathroom. Elizabeth jumped in the car in her nightgown

163

and barefoot and drove to Allen's house to tell him to get the fire truck. Quite a bit of excitement that they don't care to relive.

Albert and Elizabeth celebrated their 50th wedding anniversary August 14, 1995 with many family and friends. Still enjoying their work and their life and loving every minute of it. Albert's brother Reuben wrote a poem in 1934 that sums up the way they all felt about the ranch.

Where the mighty Pit River Flows,
And the green alfalfa grows,
Where the Double H cattle roam,
On the Modoc range near home,
Where the Shasta wind blows free,
In a valley that is fertile you'll see,
This is where I've longed to be,
For its Home Sweet Home to me.

Glorianne Weigand
December 10, 1995

Allen, Stephen, Albert, Elizabeth and Cara Lynn.

Herefords, a Family Tradition

"WAR WOLF", is the meaning of Bidwell in Norfolk County, England where the present Bidwell clan originated from in 1636. Hard workers, dedicated cattlemen and ranchers and admirable people is the meaning of Bidwell in the Hat Creek area of Shasta County in California today. The name is synonymous with the Hereford cattle breed.

In 1841 the Bidwell-Bartleson party became the first organized group of American settlers to travel to California by land. A monument at Rock Spring, Wyoming states that the Bidwell-Bartleson party were the first pioneer wagon train to pass that trail. Entering California through the Sonora Pass they came into Sutters Fort. John Horace Bidwell and his cousin the renowned Captain John Bidwell of Chico, were members of that wagon train. Moving north Captain John Bidwell settled in Chico where he built his home, the famous Bidwell Mansion that is still a prominent land mark in Chico today.

John Horace moved on to Shasta County with his wife Matilda. He was a wagon maker and blacksmith. Most of their children were born in Wisconsin. When the family traveled with their covered wagon north through the Sacramento Valley they arrived at the Anderson Ferry. It was not running, so John H. spent two days repairing it so the wagons could pass over it. They went on to Clear Creek where their last horse died. They walked on to One Horsetown carrying the baby and what supplies they could and drove the milk cow. One of their sons, William James Bidwell was eight years old at the time.

John had a blacksmith shop at Horsetown and built rocking type wagons with leather springs. It has been said that he may have been the inventor of the leather springs used on the stagecoaches. The family moved to Old Shasta, still making their living wagon making and blacksmithing. The family moved to Millville in 1869 when the father John died. His son William J. carried on the family business of blacksmithing. In 1871 William took Mary Ann Harrington as his bride.

In 1885 the Bidwell family moved to Burney. Their six year old son died the day after they arrived and their baby girl died the next month.

William Bidwell and his brother Christopher Bidwell purchased a store from their brother-in-law Charlie Teel.

While they were owners of the store they did a lot of trading with the Indians. One of the Indian Chiefs was Shavehead Bob. Shavehead was feared by many white men as well as the Indians as he was known to kill more men than any other Indian. Shavehead ran quite a bill up at the Bidwell store in Burney. When it was time for him to pay old Dave Brown and Shavehead went up by Mt. Lassen. It was the days before Mt. Lassen erupted. Old Shavehead and Dave Brown moved a big rock away from a hole in the ground. It was a large cave and Shavehead went down into the cave and returned with two sacks of gold nuggets. The Indians paid Bidwell off at the store then bought booze with the rest and went on a big party. It was believed that they stole the gold off of prospectors that they might have killed.

Mr. Wilcox, a neighboring rancher got along well with Shavehead because he paid the Indian for his land instead of trying to steal it like many settlers had.

William and Mary Ann (Harrington) Bidwell, wedding picture, 1871.

When H.G. Williams took a picture of Shavehead the other Indians told him that Shavehead would try to kill him. He thought the photographer carried bad spirits because he could make an image of the ageing Indian. That night the old Chief did come back to kill Williams, but the man had feared for his life and he was waiting for his attacker with a loaded gun. There were no shots exchanged and Williams life was spared. Old Shavehead did meet his maker over at Deer Flat sometime later.

In 1888 the two Bidwell families moved to Rising River. They traded their store in Burney to Eugene Baimbridge for his 600 acre place at Rising River. The Bidwells started raising cattle and horses. The ranch contained meadows, grain and pasture land and a fine apple orchard.

The Indian Rancheria was just across Rising River from the Bidwells. William was very fond of the Indians. He allowed them to hunt and fish on his property. Some of the Indians were Buckskin Jack who was chief, his children, Archie, Annie, Kise and Billy. Old Deerhook, Charlie Snook, McGary and Greely, Dave Brown and his wife Sarah, Joe and Annie Wilson, Lazy George, Fat Frank and Big Sam. Kate was the Bidwell's washer woman.

Big Sam was a real tall Indian and he presided over the Indian funerals. It was a sad time when one of the young Indian braves died. One funeral that was heart breaking for the Bidwells as well as the Indians, was that of young Jerry Brown, son of Dave and Sarah Brown. The Indians danced around the coffin for three days chanting as they shuffled with their arms linked to each other. When one would drop of exhaustion, another would take his place. They buried young Jerry with his saddle, saddle blanket and gun.

The Indians called William Bidwell Mr. Billy and his son little Billy.

One night Mary Ann heard a noise in the yard. With her lantern she went out to see what it was. As she raised her lantern the faces of all the Mahalies (Indian women) young boys and girls shown in the light. Mary Ann asked Old Louise what was the trouble, she replied, "Mrs. Billy, we scared as hell, Shavehead coming". Shavehead was a mean old Indian, he just as soon kill an Indian as a white man, and they were terrified of him.

The soldiers had come to look for Shavehead and the Indian Bucks and Braves had taken to the rocks hiding from the soldiers. Billy asked if they had any matches with them and finding out that they did not, he told them they could hide in the barn. When one of the Bidwell men entered the barn to care for his horses, Indian heads popped out from under the hay all over the barn.

The Indians were very devoted to the Bidwell families. In 1899, on the night Billy Bidwell died, a young Indian ran from Rising River to the

The Bidwells home at Rising River. Jim, Burney, Mac, William, John, Nellie, Anna, Mattie, Mary Ann, teacher, Irene, Lizzie, Will.

present Wilcox ranch on upper Hat Creek to get John who was working cattle there.

After Billy died, Mary Ann and the children moved closer to Cassel on the present Geissner place. The Rising River ranch was a big swamp and a lot of cattle were lost in the bogs. Mary Ann sold the cattle to buy another ranch that is now the present Floyd Bidwell and family ranch. The property Mary Ann bought was known as "Poverty Flat", but she used commercial fertilizer to bring it in to production. The land had to be cleared of timber, brush and rocks to be the productive place it is today.

Old Dave Brown and his wife Sarah stayed with the Bidwells and helped them. Dave felt it was his duty to look after Mr. Billy's little boy Mac since he wasn't yet three years old when his father Billy Bidwell died of consumption.

Charles McKinley (Mac) Bidwell was born in 1896 on the Rising River ranch. He was the youngest of eleven children of William and Mary Ann Bidwell. His other brothers and sisters were Lottie, John, William G., Burt, James, Dollie, Burney, Nellie, Lillian, and Mattie.

Mary Ann moved her family to the present Bidwell ranch. The family had a few milk cows and they kept the heifers from the dairy herd and bred them with good bulls to start a herd of beef cows. The Diamond Y brand is one of the oldest in California and was registered to Mary Ann Bidwell and sons. The family all worked hard, raising a big garden, sheep and cows. Clearing the land was a never ending project.

In 1910 when Mac was fourteen years old he was on the Hat Creek baseball team with friends and neighbors. Jim Yeaky, Benton Yeaky, Alva Opdyke, Charles Opdyke, Alan Brown, Perry Opdyke, Harry Lonquist and Ralph Bidwell. The young men had to ride horseback to Fall River or Burney to play ball.

Mac helped Mr. Brown drive cattle to Anderson, Calif. to ship them. Along the way one of the stage stops and a stop for the cattle drives was the Haynes ranch at the foot of Hatchet Mountain south west of Burney. Mr. Haynes had a twenty-two year old daughter, Birdie that took the eye of the twenty-four year old Mac Bidwell. A perfect match was made, and December 16, 1920 Mac and Birdie borrowed a buggy from Dave Doyel and went to Redding to be married. They boarded the train and took a trip to Chico for their honeymoon.

After Mac and Birdie returned from their honeymoon trip they settled themselves at the ranch where Mac had lived since he was twelve years old. They worked the ranch with Mac's mother Mary Ann. Mrs. Bidwell was caring for the children of her son William Greene Bidwell, (Little Billy). His wife Lizzie (Farmer) Bidwell had died of childbirth with her third child. The baby lived and the three children, Marie, Harold and Grace were raised by their Grandmother.

Several of Mac's sisters became teachers. Irene taught at Pollack, Nellie taught at the Island School, Lottie taught at Centerville and Burney taught at Dana. Some of them drove a wagon to their schools while others boarded with families of their pupils.

Billy Bidwell became a Forest Ranger in the Hat Creek area. His only companion was his saddle horse when he spent long hours on the trail checking the cattle for the ranchers and hauling water by pack horses to the lookout stations. Once in a while there was an old cabin that he could stay in, but most of the time he just camped on the trail. When his son Harold was old enough he took him along for the summer trips. This instilled a life long love of horses for young Harold, even though later in life he was in one of the first classes to graduate from Moler Barber College and spent his life as a barber in the Intermountain area. Harold loved to tell stories of chasing wild horses and it was always a joke that the haircut didn't end until the story did.

Mac was left to run the ranch with his mother Mary Ann. His wife Birdie loved to work in the outdoors. She loved irrigating and chopping weeds the most and took this as a serious job until she was eighty years old.

Mac and Birdie raised their family of four girls and one boy and they all took a part in working on the ranch. Maxine, Floyd, Marjorie, Virginia and Joanne.

When Floyd was three years old he was one of the many children in the area that was stricken with polio. The family was quarantined for a month. It was during lambing time and a neighbor could come and check the sheep and leave supplies for them. They had been shipping a lot of cream, but they were not able to do that during the quarantine, so that pay check was stopped.

While Mac and Birdie had to take Floyd to the hospital in San Francisco, Harold and Adelle Bidwell and their son Gene and Clarence and Goldie Hawkins and their son Norman came to stay the winter at the ranch to feed the cows and stay with the other children.

Maxine and Marjorie were the housekeepers and cooks, while Floyd, Virginia and Joanne were the ranch hands. Birdie and Mac raised a big garden. Floyd can remember they raised lots of onions and even sold some of them, there was about three acres of potatoes. The older Indians would all come to Mac in the winter and ask for some potatoes, onions and a side of bacon. Mac never turned them away. There was no welfare in those days and he would not let them go hungry. With the venison that they killed, they could eat very well on the stews they made. A lot of

Indians from Dixie Valley would ride over the rim and bring some good horses with them. Some of those families that Mac looked after were the Bones, Barnes and Mullens.

When Mary Ann died the Bidwells had to sell a lot of their cattle to settle the estate. They went in to the sheep business which was a big disaster for the family. Because of the volcanic area they live in the selenium is very deficient. They also suspected overeating disease to be the reason the lambs would die. Today both of these problems are controlled with vaccinations, but in those days it was unheard of.

When Floyd was quite young his Dad hung a gunny sack over a saddle and cut holes in it for Floyd to use as stirrups. Floyd loved to ride and still does today. When Floyd was 5 years old he would spend all summer on the trail with his Great Uncle Criss. They would move the bulls around and salt the cattle for the cattlemen. They would be up and hit the trail before daylight. Uncle Criss would be up at 3 A.M. to start breakfast and Floyd couldn't quite understand why they had to start so early, but they wanted to have their days ride in before it got too hot. Floyd said it was one of the best times of his life. It was Floyd's job to catch the horses the night before that they were going to use. Some times there would be an old cabin they would camp in, but most of the time there was not.

The Bidwell children went to school at the Lincoln school at Hat Creek. Their mother Birdie would drive them in their old car. There were more Indians at the Lincoln School than white children. But when they went to Fall River to high school, most of the young Indian boys quit to go to work in the logging operations or on ranches.

When Floyd was a sophomore in high school he had a dynamic Ag. teacher, Jesse Bequett that insisted that every boy had a project. He got Floyd interested in a Hereford beef breeding project. Floyd bought his first registered heifer from Charlie Hufford. Each time Floyd got a little money he would buy another heifer from other prominent breeders in the Hereford industry. Floyd had to change his brand and put a bar under the Diamond Y to distinguish his registered cattle from his dad's commercial herd.

Floyd's cousin Gene Bidwell worked on the ranch in the summer time and he and Gene would ride a lot together. One time Mac had found a bull up on the range that was late getting in. He told Gene and Floyd they would have to go after the bull the next day. The next morning the young cowboys saddled up and were ready to head out. Gene was riding his favorite horse Diamond who could handle most any thing. But Floyd was riding a young colt. It was hot so Birdie gave the boys some ice in a quart jar tied in a gunny sack so they would have some cool water. Floyd started to tie it on his colt, but the colt was pretty nervous about it. Gene said he would take the water, but Floyd said the horse had to learn sooner or later. Well, you may as well of tied a rattlesnake on that colt, because when that ice rattled he went to bucking and dumped Floyd in a heap. Floyd hurt his shoulder pretty bad, so Gene had to make the days ride by himself, even though he did not find the bull.

Floyd started running the ranch before his Dad died in 1962. Floyd bought an old caterpillar and cleared a lot of land. He bought several other ranches to add to the original Bidwell ranch and now has an operation that will run around 1200 female cows.

Floyd and Gene helped drive 1000 head of 800 pound steers to Cottonwood in the 40's to load on the train.

It was snowing hard and they had to camp out, The dogs tried to crawl in to Gene's sleeping bag to keep warm and Floyd had a horse wreck that cut his head quite severely. It was all in a days work of young cowboys on the trail.

Floyd started showing his cattle at the county fair and different places and he and Gene had quite a time.

Today the Bidwell cattle are still in the show ring at the prominent Bull Sales.

The Bidwell girls left home for school and to later be married. Maxine married Floyd Summers and they have two children, Virginia married Corky DeAtley and they have five children, Marjorie married Lem Earnest and they had two children and Joanne married Clark Wolf and they have three children. Floyd married Ethel Martin from Elko, Nevada and they have three children.

The Red Bluff Bull Sale is a part of life for the busy Bidwell family. The Bidwell bulls use to be shown at many bull sales including, the Reno Nugget, Klamath Falls, Cow Palace, Stockton, Ferndale and Sacramento.

In 1941 several Red Bluff cattlemen got together and decided that they needed to have a bull sale there and have breeders bring their bulls to them rather than they have to go all over the country looking for bulls. The first year Floyd had three bulls at that sale, and in fifty-five years there was only one sale that he missed with his bulls, and that is because there was such a blizzard that he could not get there.

Many many times the Bidwells have had champion pens of five and champion pens of three at that prominent sale. Some of the cattlemen that have purchased those pen lots were the Boston Ranch, Roy Nicholson, Roger Nicholson, Jack Owens, Russ Cattle Co., Ed Osburn, Bob Byrnes, Laxague, Hyde Ranch, Orem Ranch and Bill Owens. These are just some of the buyers that have bought the most pen lots from the Bidwell Herefords.

Floyd Bidwell, 1967.

In 1979 Bidwells averaged $3,450.00 for the thirty-five bulls they took to Red Bluff. That was the best year they ever had.

Floyd use to raise up to two hundred bulls, but now they only raise about fifty. Of those they use about twenty themselves, the Porterfield ranch always buys bulls at the ranch. The Bidwells only take bulls to the Red Bluff sale now.

Artificial insemination practices are used on the ranch on about one hundred and fifty pure bred cows and on some of the better commercial cows.

The calf crop from the ranch is marketed in several different areas. Right now there are two hundred steers on feed at Red Oak, Iowa at a feedlot and they are gaining 4.05 pounds a day. When they left the ranch at Hat Creek in September they weighed 840 and they are now at 1200 pounds in 97 days. They will be processed there. This is a certified Hereford Beef program. Sometimes the cattle are sold on the video sale and also to individual buyers.

Most of the cattle are sent south to the valley to spend the winter. The calves gain really well on the green grass. The Bidwells own a place near Cottonwood and they also rent a lot of pasture.

The winter of 1993 a lot of snow fell in Northern California and two hundred of Bidwell's cattle were stranded on Bald Mountain in two feet of snow. The only way to get to them was by a caterpillar so they could get hay to them. Floyd froze his feet while driving the cat the long slow miles. But like most cattlemen, you think of your cows first then take care of yourself.

The cattle are trucked backed to the ranch around the first part of May then they are sent to the Forest Service and Bureau of Land Management ranges for the summer.

The Bidwell Ranch has been named "Seedstock Producer of the year for 1995".

In 1985 the ranch started a new project that has been very successful. They built a hydro electric plant which was a series of three stations at a cost of ten million dollars. Lost creek is the creek that supplies the ranch with its abundance of water. With much planning, hard work and ingenuity the dream came true. The plants, Lost Creek #1 produced 1400 KWH, #2 is a little less than that, but what they call the Bidwell Ditch Project has a fall of 500 feet and produces 2,000 KWH. This electricity is sold to P.G.& E. It took one year to build each plant project.

With the fall of the water there is an excess of oxygen in the water. This is the perfect environment to raise fish. They do not even have to move their gills to breath they can just lay there and get fat. The average two year old trout weighs fifteen pounds. A fish in their feeding ponds will gain a pound on a pound of food. The fish are shipped all over California by Mt. Lassen Trout Farms to stock some thirty lakes.

The water that starts from springs in the Hat Creek rim and is known as Lost Creek is used eleven times before it leaves the Bidwell property. The water runs through three power stations to make electricity, two feeder fish ponds, four fishing ponds for fly fisherman that have the rights leased, stock water and irrigating of the hay fields. It then goes back into the Hat Creek Rim. Fishing is allowed year around on private lakes, so there is an abundance of travel through the Bidwell Ranch.

A few years ago a mountain lion was seen going up the steep bluff near the ranch with a hundred pound newborn calf in its mouth. The children play near where the calf was taken from. They figure that the mountain lion kills a deer a day. The deer herd has greatly diminished in that area and the lions are on the increase.

L. to R.: Abner McKenzie, Floyd Bidwell, Mark Bidwell, David Spooner, Jim Earnest, Lem Earnest, Bill Verdigo, Sam Thurber, Bill Owens. Champion Pen of 5 Red Bluff Bull Sale, 1973.

The Bidwells do all of their own haying with the exception of hauling most of it. They did have 66,000 bales hauled this past year by a contractor.

The Bidwells appreciate their good dogs, good horses and good bulls.

The Bidwell Ranch is a family operation and Mark and Ross and their families are carrying on the traditions of bulls at the Red Bluff Bull Sale.

Ross married Peggy Cannavan and they have Marty, Lindsey and Chad. Mark married Debbie Davies and they have Blair, Bliss and Bailey. Cindy married Mike Songer and they have Tanner and Wade. All the children are involved in rodeos, and driving cattle on the ranch. The love of horses and livestock has been instilled in all of the family. All the grandchildren of Floyd and his sister Virginia are involved with the Jr. Rodeo at McArthur. As soon as they are old enough to sit in the saddle they are riding. Even the Great Grandson of Harold Bidwell had that love passed on to him as well as the DeAtley children. As it is said, born to ride fits these little cowboys and cowgirls.

As long as there are bulls on the Bidwell Ranch you can bet there will be a Bidwell Bull in the ring until the auctioneer hollers, "SOLD".

Glorianne Weigand
January 15, 1996

Notches on Their Sling Shots

Notches on your gun is one thing for a gun slinger, but notches on your sling shot, now that's a different story. But for two young brothers David and Bob Schneider, who were crack shots, that is how they kept track of the apple eating birds they killed that would invade the family's orchard. The birds in the apple trees along with the squirrels in the grain field were also the target for the two young hunters. The boys made their sling shots by whittling a forked oak limb and using a rubber band from an old inner tube. A piece of leather from an old shoe would complete their sling shots. Their younger brother Asa tells that they would carve a notch in the fork for each bird they killed and he tells that he can remember over ninety notches in a fork then they would have to build a new one. The young boys carried so many rocks in their pockets that their legs got sore. Bob traded for an old muzzle loader bullet mold and poured round lead balls for their ammunition. He would melt down the lead out of old batteries for this purpose. Traps and .22 Rifles were also used to keep the varmints out of the crops.

These two young marksmen were third generation members of the Schneider family of Day, Modoc County in North Eastern California. This community is also known as Little Hot Springs Valley. David and Bobby along with their other brothers and sisters, Charles (Chick), Viola (Tiny), Eugene, Amy, LaVella, Asa and Freda were the children of Fred and Viola Schneider.

Fred who was born near Anderson, California in 1883 was the son of David and Amy Schneider. He had two sisters, Viola and Sophy, and one brother Johnnie. In 1888 David and Amy loaded their wagons and hired a drover to drive their cattle and moved through Whitmore, over Tamarack Road, down through Burney, on to Fall River Mills and on to Little Hot Springs Valley. David bought a two hundred acre ranch that had been homesteaded by George Bean and had been sold to John McAfee. Soon after they settled on their new ranch Johnnie died at the age of seven from typhoid fever. A year later in the winter of 1889-90 another daughter

Alice was born. Fred remembered this being one of the hardest winters in history. The ground was covered with five feet of snow from early November and the ground was never seen until April the next spring.

David bought another parcel from a neighbor, Jake Seiger and added this 80 acres to his ranch. Many hot springs bubble up in the valley, thus giving it the name Little Hot Springs Valley. Another portion of the ranch was acquired by paying off a mortgage for a friend and with an extra payment to him David purchased that ranch. A patent from the U.S. Government of 160 acres in 1904 brought the total acreage of the Schneider ranch to 320 acres.

The many hot springs in the valley were wonderful for mineral baths when the water had a chance to cool some and it was hot enough to scald hogs on butchering day. Watermelons were planted near the hot springs and sub irrigated from the hot water. The Schneiders claim they were the sweetest and biggest melons ever grown. They were hauled by the wagon load to Big Valley and to Fall River Valley by the Schneiders and later by Arch Hollenbeak who purchased the hot springs ranch from David in 1909 and later the Walter Lorenzen family raised watermelon there until 1940.

In 1903 when Fred was twenty years old he went out to do the morning chores and never came back in. There had been a family argument and he just disappeared. It was quite some time later that he wrote a letter to Annie Lorenzen and told her he was in Washington. When he got mad hc just walkcd cross country to Bartlc and caught a train and decided it was time to get out on his own. He was working on railroad bridges there. A couple years later he returned a much wiser man, and some of the experience building the bridges came in handy for his future occupation of barn builder. Fred ran the ranch for his mother Amy and a couple years later in 1907 he bought the ranch from her.

David and Amy had separated and David had kept the hot springs ranch which he sold to Hollenbeak. In 1909 David moved to McArthur and bought a livery stable. A lively business that was located right next to the McArthur canal, but in 1918 when the automobile became popular he was forced to close his business as those autos passed the livery stable right by.

Fred was busy running the ranch at Day. He had a small herd of cattle that he branded with the FS brand. He branded his horses with the FS bar. It took a lot of horses to plow the fields and work the farm. Fred raised quite a bit of grain for his hogs and chickens and to sell or take to the mill at Fall River to trade for their year supply of flour. Fred and some neighbors Hi and Walter Lorenzen went in to a partnership and bought a grain thrasher. From 1910 to 1919 they took their thrasher from ranch to ranch and thrashed grain for other farmers in Little Hot Springs Valley and Fall River Valley.

In 1914 Fred bought his first car, a 1914 Maxwell, he was really proud of the two seated convertible. In 1915, Fred, Asa Hollenbeak, George Handley, Mary Hollenbeak and Belle Hollenbeak packed their suit cases and headed to the San Francisco Fair.

As Fred traveled to and from Redding in his new car he would often stop at Ingot to buy gas for his vehicle. A young gal took his eye when they met. Viola Rogers was the daughter of the foreman of the carpenter crew on the Terry Mill lumber flume. Viola and her family had moved there from Pittsburg, California where she was born in 1896. Fred and Viola went to Redding to be married November 27, 1915. Fred was thirty-two years old and Viola was nineteen. The newlyweds returned to the ranch at Day to settle down to a bustling married life and a house full of kids.

All of the children of Fred and Viola were all born at home with a neighbor or midwife to tend to the mother and baby. A new baby joined the family every two years. Chick, 1916; Tiny, 1918; Eugene, 1920; Bobbie, 1922; Amy, 1924; David, 1926; LaVella, 1928; Asa, 1932 and Freda, 1935. This was quite a family when all the washing had to be done by hand. All the diapers plus all of the rest of the washing had to be scrubbed on a scrub board in water that was pumped by hand and heated in a large cast iron pot that held thirty of gallons. The large pot hung over the fire in the yard to heat the water, it then was dipped out and carried to the wash house for the laundry to be done. On wash day an Indian lady, Mariah Williams came to help with the washing. She washed for several different families in the area.

A gasoline driven washing machine was bought in 1926. Viola thought this was a wonderful invention. There was no electricity at the remote ranch until 1968. Kerosene lamps, wood stoves and packing your water was a way of life and no one expected anything different.

Viola baked seven loaves of bread every other day to feed her family. School lunches had to be made and at times others boarded with the family and that was extra mouths to feed. All the meals for the large family were made from what was grown on the ranch. Two large gardens were raised in the fertile valley in the summer. Large apple and pear orchards provided them with fruit. Many jars of fruit, vegetables, jams, pickles, catsup, and meat were canned. The main meat for the family was pork as it could be cured and smoked to keep it. The hogs were butchered at the Hot Springs where the water bubbled out of the ground at 170 degrees, just right for scalding hogs. As many as ten hogs at a time were butchered to feed the large family. It had to be done in the cool winter months so the meat

Fred and Viola Schneider, 1943.

would cool out. There were always chickens to butcher. When deer season came around the family would really smile because there would be a change of meat on the table. At that time you were able to kill two deer and when each of the boys got their tags there was an abundance of venison for the family. There were always at least one hundred and fifty deer in the apple orchard every night through the summer. Armed with a shotgun, the boys would camp down there to keep the deer from eating all the apples and the garden.

The girls can remember their butterflies. Freda had thirty-nine monarch butterflies in a box. Every day she would pick fresh milkweed for them. One day over three hundred butterflies hatched from the box and filled the air with beautiful butterflies.

The Schneider family was a close knit loving family and still are today. They really never wanted for anything. The store house was full of food that they had grown and preserved themselves. Their mother made most of their clothes, but the Montgomery Ward and Sears Roebuck Catalogs were a very important part of their life. They ordered what clothes and shoes they needed. The mail was delivered two times a week at the little Day post office and it would not take long for their orders to be received.

The family only went to town two or three times a year to get the supplies they needed. Grain was traded for flour and Fred would bring fifty sacks of 50 pounds of flour and stack it in the store room along with the other supplies. The root cellar held the potatoes, onions, carrots, parsnips and cabbage. A five gallon can of honey and a five gallon can of syrup were there to top off their mothers wonderful biscuits and pancakes.

Winters were harsh in the mountains of Modoc County so school was not held in December, January and February. The snow was too deep for the children to walk the two and a half miles to school any way. School was held all summer with a short vacation in the middle. The boys had to help with the haying on the weekend and the girls had to help with chores and the garden. Every child had their chores to do. Even when they were very small they would have chores. Eugene can remember when he was quite small and had to gather the eggs. There was a tall board at the bottom of the door to the chicken house. He made it over the board all right to get into the chicken house with his egg bucket empty. But getting out was another problem. He thought he could throw the bucket up in the air, jump over the board and catch the bucket before it landed. Either he didn't throw the bucket high enough or he didn't jump fast enough, because the eggs landed before he caught them, and he had a scrambled mess.

The school at Day was a one room school and there would be from twelve to twenty kids with one teacher. Some of the teachers were Frances Gassaway, Bertha Riley, Joe Steele, Phoebe Lorenzen, Rose Joiner, Thelma Estes and Virginia Speers. The Oiler family was a large family also and had many children in the school as well as the Lorenzen, Harvey, Layton and Wertz. Favorite games at school were marbles, hop scotch, ball games and Annie Annie Over.

When it was time for Amy to go to high school she had to go to Adin as she lived in Modoc County and had to attend school in that county. She boarded with Dr. Smith and his wife.

In 1930 an airplane flew in to the valley and landed which was quite a thrill for everyone.

Winters were a fun time for the Schneider children even though they were snowed in. They would take nice straight grain boards off of the horse manger in the barn to make ski's and sleds. They made sure they replaced the ones they took. Snow forts, snow ball fights, reading books, helping their mother make quilts, fun and games filled the winter months. There was never time to be bored.

Christmas was a special time for the family. When the Sears and Wards catalogs were delivered the children would start their shopping and wish lists. They knew there would not be a lot of gifts with such a

Late 1930's. Top: Hi Lorenzen. Front: Fred Schneider, Walt Lorenzen, Bob Schneider, with their grain thresher.

Winter meat supply. Asa, Dave and (Dad) Fred Schneider.

large family, so they took their time and chose their presents carefully. The order was sent and Santa was expected to bring the gifts they asked for. Viola made night gowns and pajamas for each of the children and stuffed animals. She spent many hours at her treadle sewing machine keeping the family clothes made and mended, also making clothes and diapers for a new baby every two years. A hard working and caring woman, but never a complaint was heard.

Fred would go to the hills to get their Christmas tree. It was always a cedar tree as the fir trees were too far up the mountain to expect one of those. The children would make ornaments and string popcorn to go along with the other ornaments in the Christmas box. Small metal holders were placed on the tree that held little candles. On Christmas Eve the candles were lit and everyone sat around the tree watching the candles glow. They would have to be watched carefully so they would not catch the tree on fire.

Chick was the oldest of the family and soon began to realize there was no Santa Clause so he took great pride in making things out of wood for his brothers and sisters. He was quite clever, A small table and chairs, doll beds and wooden toys were the gifts he made.

One time an elderly Indian lady, Gracie Wolfin came to the Schneiders to buy some flour. She asked Viola, "When you going to present and candy them children?" "I like to come." She was invited to share in the family Christmas celebration. Viola made her an apron and made sure there were a couple of gifts under the tree for her. Tiny can still remember the smile on her face and her eyes shining with happiness as she shared the family's holiday.

A highlight in the family life was when the traveling salesman for the Watkins Company paid his yearly visit in his old Model T Ford. His name was Mr. Sackville and he always brought the children chewing gum. It was the only gum they ever had. Mr. Sackville would always spend the night with the Schneider family and they would purchase their years supply of liniment, cold tablets, salve, vanilla and spices. He always commented on how well all the children behaved.

In 1910 Fred had met a man that would teach him a very valuable trade. John Wilderman taught Fred how to hew timbers and frame round poles for barn construction. He helped Fred build a barn on his ranch. Learning to build barns was an excellent skill and turned into a good business for the young farmer. Fred was a craftsman and he built thirteen barns in the Day, Fall River and Big Valley area, and many of them still are in use today. He also built smaller buildings such as granaries, machine sheds, chicken and hog houses.

In 1932 Fred built the Hi Lorenzen barn in Day, in 1936 he built a large barn for Tom Barrows in Round Valley East of Adin. At that time Tiny had been going to school in Susanville and staying with family friends. When Fred built the barn at the Barrows ranch Mrs. Barrows was looking for a helper to cook for the hay crew so Tiny worked there for that summer. In 1937 Fred built a large barn in downtown Pittville for Arch Hollenbeak. In 1939 two barns were built on the Albaugh ranch. One still stands right next to the highway and the other burned when the hay caught fire. In 1943 a barn was built for Vernon Royce. In 1946 he dismantled and moved and reconstructed a barn for the Crum Meat Company and in 1947 he built two more barns for them. While building a barn for his son-in-law Baldy McCully lightning hit Fred's barn in Little Hot Springs Valley and it burned. He built another barn for himself on his place in 1949, that was the last barn he built. The first and last barns he built were for himself.

The barns that Fred built were a real work of art and something he was very proud of. Every one was perfect. As his sons grew older they worked on the barns with him. The first chore was to go to the mountains and choose the timber to be used. He would search and search for just the right log for just the right location in the project. Whether it was the pole for the north east corner or the one for the middle of the barn. They had to be just perfect and each one was chosen for a specific location. The timbers were hauled by team and wagon to the job site and the bark was peeled from the log.

The lumber was hauled by team and wagon from Gooch mill on Big Valley Mountain. The logs were all cut to fit and the ends were shaped. The frame was built on the ground and a team of horses, a long line and a gin pole were used to raise the sides into place. Besides his sons helping him there were usually a man or two on the place he was working that would help with the construction.

In 1918 Fred bought a new Maxwell car and took the family for a drive to Chico, Calif. where he bought a Kissel truck. It took two full days to drive home from Chico, one hundred and fifty miles. It was dirt and mud all the way as it was in November.

Before Fred bought his new truck the hogs had to be driven cross country to the nearest railroad at Bartle. A long hard drive that took several days. In 1920 after Fred got his new Kissel he left the ranch one day to haul a load of hogs to market for a neighbor. Ten days later he finally returned one evening and walked in to the house and ask, "what's for dinner." Viola told him that maybe he had better go back and bring her a box of candy or something for being gone so long. He handed her two hundred dollars that he had made hauling freight and flour from the

Crieghton warehouse and flour mill at Glenburn to Big Valley and Bartle, and freight back to Fall River Valley.

When the depression years of 1929 and 1930 hit the ranch could not quite make a living for such a large family so Fred went to work in saw mills and logging in the woods in the summer and built barns in the winter

Fred worked for Zamboni at his mill near Lookout by the Great Northern Railroad tracks from 1933 to 1935. He then went to work for Gooch Lumber Company when they started a mill at Day. Fred worked there until 1946. In 1936 his two oldest sons, Chick and Gene were both working for Gooch Lumber. Bob also went to work there as soon as he was old enough. The boys were working in the mill by the time they were sixteen years old. Beginning a life of work in the timber industry for some of them.

In 1941 Gene went into the Army. In 1942 Chick went into the Air Force. In 1942 Bob went into the Army and was killed in Italy right at the end of the war. He was twenty-two years old. In 1945 David went in

50th wedding anniversary of Fred and Viola Schneider, 1965. Back row: David, Asa, Eugene and Chick. Front row: Amy, Tiny, Viola, Fred, LaVella, Freda.

to the Army. Asa went in to the Air Force in 1951. All of the boys served their time for their country.

After the service Chick and Gene ran a logging operation for Gooch. They then went to work for PG&E. After David finished helping his Dad build barns he started falling timber for Finny Logging Co. of Bieber.

Chick was married to Ruth Burkholder and they had no children. Chick passed away in 1983.

Gene married Joy Reynolds and they had three children. After she passed away he married Dora Babcock Carpenter. Tiny married Glen Hollenbeak and they had three children. Tiny later married Art Williams and after he passed away she married Boss Hawkins. Amy married Baldy McCully and they had five children. LaVella married Daly Lee and they have two daughters. Freda married Bill Murphy and they have three children. David married Rose Agee and they have four children. Asa married Helen McCutchen and they have four children.

The family of Fred and Viola Schneider included nine children. twenty-four grandchildren, thirty-six great grandchildren and eight great-great grandchildren.

In later years when several of the family had left home Christmas had changed. This was the day that their Dad Fred decided to butcher eight or ten hogs. The weather was cool and everyone came for dinner and a visit, so why not take advantage of the help. Viola always scraped and cleaned all the gut for the casings for the sausage. A long hard tedious job.

The little community of Day was a close knit fun place to raise a big family. Dances were held every Saturday night at the community hall and the Bosworth Trio from Cayton Valley would come to play.

Fred sold the ranch in Little Hot Springs Valley June 16, 1968. Just eighty years to the day of the time the Schneiders first bought the ranch. Fred and Viola moved to McArthur and lived the rest of their lives there. They had been married fifty-five years. They were loved deeply by their family and their granddaughter Sally McCully wrote this poem about her grandmother. Viola never had the poem read to her as she passed away right after it was written.

She is my Mama's Mama
And an Angel in my eyes
One of Gods most precious gifts
I've come to realize
She can tell you stories
that'll bring tears to your eyes,

She's gentle, kind and loving
and from experience, very wise.
Her childhood was a rough one
she remembers to this day.
Then Grandpa came into her life
and pushed the clouds away.
Together they raised their children
on the ranch they owned in Day
life was never easy
But she had the strength to stay.
As I load my new dishwasher
I think of how it was back then
She had to heat the water first,
then slip the dishes in.
Everything was fresh from scratch
and time consuming too.
But the love she had for her family
made it all easier to do.
I'd like to have her recipes,
for the cookies, pies and bread,
but their not written anywhere,
they are stored there in her head.
Time has slowed her down some
she now has to use a walker,
but sit her down, one on one.
and she becomes a talker.
And listen close to what she says.
cause she has so much to offer
advise on life and raising kids,
and the perfect spice cake toppers.
But now I add a final verse
to this story I have told
Grandma you'll always be in my heart,
And your memory I will hold.
I'll tell my children's, children,
about a lady so rare,
And hope that I can instill in them
how Grandma taught me to care.

Glorianne Weigand
February 5, 1996

Gold Coins in a Tree Stump

Milk those cows, feed those chickens and hogs, get that harvesting done. It's time to change the sprinklers or bale that hay. That's the way things go on the Al and Nelda Bruce ranch in McArthur. Along the Pit River is some beautiful bottom land. The green rolling hills in the spring with the grain sprouting and the golden sheaves waving in the breeze in the fall just before harvest.

A busy ranch with a family working together. Al and Nelda's son Ernest and his wife Joanne (Dotson) live in the original home of Joe Bruce and raised their three children Brian, Pamela and Kathy there. Like Ernest's Grandparents, Joe and Arie Bruce raised their children in the same house. Edward was born in 1912, Jim in 1914, Albert in 1917, Bob in 1919 and Norma in 1926.

Of Scottish ancestry young Joe Bruce arrived in New York at the age of twenty-one. The trip by boat from Aberdeen, Scotland took two weeks. Joe had left his parents Ernest and Annie Bruce in his homeland and never returned to see them. A brother and sister also came to the United States in later years. The year was 1906 and travel was slow. Joe then bought a train ticket to Sisson, California, (Sisson is now known as Mount Shasta). Arriving at Sisson he then loaded his belongings into a stage coach and headed to Bartle, then on to Fall River Valley. In those days you had to have a sponsor to be able to come to the United States. His sponsors were the Toescher family in McArthur, Calif. They owned a hotel and were good friends of the Ingrams. In Scotland a young man had to have a trade, and Joe was a bookkeeper and a good one. He was hired at McArthurs store and did their bookkeeping. Young Roderick McArthur and Joe became very good friends. He was tired of an inside job and Roderick hired him to work on the dredger when they were making dykes to drain the swamp. At one time the Big Lake came within a mile of McArthur and after all the dredging work it was channeled and controlled and the swamp was drained. The dykes were used to control the water and the water was channeled through the McArthur canal. The McArthurs sold water to the farmers near the Bruce ranch. Jed Crouch owned the place Al and Nelda now live and Bosworth owned what the Crum ranch was.

Joe enjoyed the dredging work and was really good at it. When he finished in the McArthur Swamp, he went to Klamath Falls, Oregon to run the dredger on Klamath Lake in 1908 and 1909. The job was to put dykes in to build the lake.

For a short time Joe was a conductor on a street car, before he returned to the McArthur area.

Charles and Alice Cathcart traveled with their family by train from Pennsylvania to California and set up their homestead in Widow Valley near Lookout, Calif. Charles died when his small daughter Arie was four years old. In a few years Alice married Mr. Wendt. They moved to his beautiful home along the Pit River.(The Wendt home is the big two story house that is now owned by Hilda Brum). Arie Cathcart was a charming young lady that took the eye of young Joe Bruce. Joe and Arie met at church at Pittville, a courtship started and ended in marriage. Joe and Arie went by horse and buggy to Alturas sixty miles away and were married on January 17, 1912 by Reverend I.C. Crook of the Congregational Church. Joe was 28 and Arie was 27.

Wedding picture, Joe Bruce and Arie Cathcart, Jan. 12, 1912.

Joe Bruce and his meat peddling wagon, 1913.

"JOE W. BRUCE BUTCHER SHOP", is the sign that hung over the little butcher shop in McArthur. Joe bought his beef and hogs from other ranchers, butchered them out then peddled it with his horse and wagon. He ran his butcher shop from 1912 to 1916, then he decided he wanted to buy a place of his own. Joe and Arie bought 120 acres from McArthurs. It was a bare piece of land, not a building nor tree in sight. Archie Wright was the carpenter that built a new home for Joe and his family in 1916. Al was the first of the children to be born in the new home. When Bob was born Joe needed to call Dr. Pratt. Being a private man he did not want every one on the telephone party line to know his business. He called the Dr. and told him Arie had a tooth ache. The Dr. knew what a prankster Joe was so he hurried on his way to deliver the new baby.

Joe built a chicken house, barns and buildings and an orchard was planted and the bare land soon became a beautiful ranch.

Joe started a dairy and called it the Beaver Creek Dairy. Milking seventeen holsteins was quite a job. The whole milk was taken to the cheese factory at McArthur that Hugh Watson was running. After the

First tractor in Fall River Valley, 1912.
Al Ferrell and George Horr hauling lumber for Grange Hall.

Nelda's Grandpa Chace logging near Shingle Town.

Watson creamery shut down, Joe then separated his milk and took the cream to the Fall River Meat Company that Mr. Royce ran.

Joe then was given the whey from the cheese and along with his own skim milk and grain he fattened out his hogs.

The Bruce children walked across the field to the Beaver Creek School. All the children from the neighboring ranches went to school there, then went on to high school at McArthur. The teachers that the Bruce children had at Beaver Creek where Pheobe Lorenzen, Mrs. Lanigan and Nellie Callison. The Bruce, Dawson, Knoch, Crum, Bean and Ingram children all went to this one room school along Peacock Creek.

Joe bought another 180 acres from Farners and Naler. There was a big cellar on this place and a lot of Indian artifacts. The local Indians had left their baskets and lots of beads at that place. Joe said he had no use for any Indian baskets, so he dumped them all in the cellar and filled in the hole, burying them.

Water was bought by the acre. It was cheaper to buy the water than to pump it even though these places bordered the Pit River. Some of the places did not have riparian rights to the river water anyhow. The price of the water got pretty high and good alfalfa hay was only selling for $5.00 a ton. The water cost more than the hay was worth. Joe Bruce was the last to give the water up.

Joe wanted to buy some milk cows and he went to William Wendt his wife's step father to borrow some money. William thought very highly of Joe and told him he would be more than happy to loan him the money. He told Joe to stay in the house and he would be right back. William was not gone long and returned with $2,000.00 in gold coins. He had them hid outside somewhere, "maybe in a tree trunk". In those days banks were not thought too highly of. Many people hid their money in strange places. Grandma Wendt must have been tucking a little away on her own and no one ever knew about it. She had made a little foot stool by covering tin cans with fabric and sewing them in a circle. Many many years later and after the home had been sold time and time again, the lady of the house got tired of the little ugly footstool in the upstairs bedroom. Everyone had moved in and out, but never took the little ugly stool with them. So, the lady of the house gave the little stool a kick and sent it sailing down the stairs. To her surprise a large amount of green backs went flying through the air. Enough was stashed away in the little stool to take a long vacation to Europe.

As the family grew up Ed went away to a diesel mechanic school at Portland, Oregon. He later worked on the building of Shasta Dam and then worked for Butte Tractor in Redding. Ed moved back to McArthur and opened the Bruce Equipment Company and raised his family, he and his wife Helen (Jarvis) had three children, Joe, David and Carol Ann. Helen passed away from leukemia when Carol Ann was only three years old. The Bruce Equipment Company is still run by Ed's son Joe today.

Jim stayed at home with his folks and worked for Royce at the Fall River Meat Co. Jim was the first man in the Fall River Valley to go to war, he was wounded several times then contacted malaria. After returning from the service, he married Pauline Bran and they had three children Gordon, Bonnie and Robbie. Jim passed away from Cancer before Robbie was born. He was only 38 years old.

After a few years Ed Bruce and his brothers widow Pauline were married combining the families and raising the six Bruce cousins as brothers and sisters.

Robert (Bob) Bruce was in the Navy during the war. In 1944 his ship was bombed and he went down with his ship when he was only twenty-five years old. Jim was in the service at the same time and from where he was stationed he could see the ships being bombed in the harbor, wondering if his brother might be on one of the ships. When he got home he found out Bob had been lost at sea.

The only girl in the Bruce family, Norma married Walter Callison, a young man from a prominent ranching family also. They went into ranching in the Glenburn area and raised their children, Bob, Marilyn, Richard and Russell.

Joe made a deal with his son Al to stay on the ranch and help him out. Al also farmed on shares for McArthurs.

Al and Jim had bought the Jed Crouch place next door to Joe and Arie in 1939. Jim Day had rented this place for twenty years or more. When Jim passed away, his daughter Ivadell and son in law Hugh Carpenter moved on to the place and took care of things for them. Hugh and Ivadell cared for her younger brothers and sisters as well as their own children.

The Bruce family were neighbors to the Crum family and by that time the children rode their bikes to school. Mrs. Farrell had come to cook for the Crum family after Mrs. Crum passed away. She had a daughter, Nelda that lived with her on the Crum ranch. Nelda rode her bike to school down the lane and had to pass the Bruce ranch. Nelda soon became acquainted with Al Bruce.

On a snowy morning with ten inches of snow on the ground, Al and Nelda took off to Reno, Nevada to get married. February 14, 1940. Seventeen year old Nelda and twenty-three year old Al along with their Mothers and Al's sister Norma and brother Jim were the wedding party that headed to the wedding chapel.

When the newly weds came back home they set up housekeeping in the place that Al and Jim had bought from Crouch. The home on the ranch had been built in 1919. There was no electricity, running water or indoor plumbing. Electricity did come into the area in 1941.

The Bruce ranch produces a lot of grain. Times have changed from teams of horses to the most modern harvester. In the early days Albert Lorenzen, Bob Ingram and Joe Bruce worked together to get their harvesting done. Bob drove the teams, Al Lorenzen ran the header and Joe sewed the sacks. Al Bruce usually hauled the sacks and lifted all of them on to the wagons until they got a loader in 1946. The loader was used to load sacks of grain then later was used for baled hay.

All of the plowing and drilling of the fields was done with teams of horses until they bought a D4 Caterpillar in 1941. Al Lorenzen bought a Caterpillar in 1940 and they used his to pull the harvester. The teams of work horses were used to mow the hay for many years.

Nelda cooked for the crews when they were working on the Bruce ranch. After the grain was harvested at the Bruce ranch they would move on to the neighbors and do their harvesting. Al Bruce and Alex Ingram broke all the teams themselves that they used. The teams were also used to haul the hay to the barns. Ropes were attached to the nets that were used to lift the hay into the barns. The hay nets are a series of boards and ropes that lay flat in the wagon and when the wagons are in the fields the loose hay is pitched into the wagon on the nets by hand. When the team and wagon get to the barn a long rope tied to a pulley at the end of the barn is lowered and attached to the rope on the nets. A single horse is used to pull the nets into the air and through the top door and down the track to where the stacker wants it to be dumped. When the stacker hollers "DUMP", a rope is pulled and the nets open from the bottom dumping the load of hay for the stacker man to pitch into the stack.

Al and Nelda's family started coming along to keep them busy. Charles was born November 1940, Ernest was born 1942 and Betty was born in 1945.

Joe had bought a few stock cows to go along with his dairy cows. He traveled to Big Valley and bought a bull and some cows from a rancher over there, Charlie Leonard. David Shaffer hauled the cattle over the hill for Al. They were good cows, but there was a problem with the bull and he had an abortion disease. This disease caused them to lose all of their calf crop. Joe had borrowed the money from the bank so this hurt the pocket book a little bit.

Al and Jim bought twelve cows from John Jensen over near Glenburn. Al, Nelda, Joe and Jim rode their horses across the valley to drive the cattle home. One cow wouldn't cross the bridge, so she swam the river.

Times have changed in the livestock industry as far as vaccinations the cows have to receive. All Joe use to vaccinate for was black leg. Scour remedies were made by boiling milk and giving that to a calf, raw eggs, or browning flour and mixing it with molasses and rolling it into little balls to put down the calves throat. One time a bunch of their sheep bloated and an old Indian told them, "they shouldn't have died, pour turpentine down them".

A good cow bloated and they used turpentine on her and it worked.

Al and Nelda's family grew up and were married. Charles, the oldest son married Aldora Bell and they had two children, Daniel and Annette. Charles moved his family to Oregon where he worked in a plywood factory. He contacted cancer and died in 1973 at the age of 31. His son Daniel works on the Bruce ranch with his Grandfather Al and Uncle Ernest.

Betty married Jim Hamilton and they live in Adin. They have two sons, Bruce and John. Bruce also works on the ranch where his mother was raised.

Al bought 240 acres from the Hawes family to add to his ranch. In 1940 Al had a chance to buy 80 acres from a neighbor for $3,500.00, but Grandpa Joe talked them out of it, thought it was too much money.

Al worked at the Crum Meat Company right down the road for years. He helped scrape hogs on butchering day and on one day they scraped 125 hogs.

After the Crum Meat Company closed down there was a chance for Al and Nelda to buy the Crum ranch. The slaughter plant had partially burned, but there were three homes on the ranch that Al and Nelda rent out. There was 155 acres of the Crum ranch that the Bruce ranch added to their own.

Al sold grain to Christensen at their feed store in Redding. They became great friends. The feed store had a drawing for a little donkey, so Nelda signed up for it. Cracker Jack was his name and Nelda won him. The kids had more fun with that little donkey.

Nelda's family came from South Cow Creek near Millville, California. Charles Farrell the father of the family died when Nelda was only eight years old. Seven children were left for his wife to care for. Virgil, Blanch, Roy, Lorita, Velma, Nelda and George To make a living for her family Annie Farrell did what she knew best, she started cooking. First it was at a logging camp at the Plum Mill at Dana. Her boys Roy and Virgil worked in the logging there. Moving around for a time she finally came to the Crum ranch in McArthur and there she was the family cook for many years. Mrs. Crum had passed away and there was a large family besides the hay crew and the crew from the slaughter plant to cook for.

The Bruce family gathering grain for the fair. Al, Charles, Ernest, Nelda and Betty.

Annie Farrell remarried Mr. Woods later in life. She passed away a year after Al and Nelda were married.

The Farrell family was well known around the Millville area, some of them are still there. Virgil married Henrietta Darrah and they had Beverly and Bud. Blanch married Buck Abbott and their children were Donald, Arthur and Donna.Roy married Marie Johnson and their children were Mary Lou, John and Ruth. Lorita married Fred Schellings and Anna Marie and Fred were their offspring. Velma married Ellis Jones and added Shirley and Richard to their family. George married Hattie Hunt and moved away to Montana with their family Bill, Peggy and Wayne.

The Farrell and Bruce families had good times with family picnics, playing horseshoes and cards. On holidays the loser in the card games had to do the dishes. Al was the loser one Thanksgiving and the dishes were his to do. He soon went to town and bought Nelda her first dishwasher.

Al had a new motorbike. He and Ernest were separating some bulls and the bulls got on the fight. Several of the grandkids were with them.

Joe and Arie Bruce and children, Ed, Al, and Norma, Jan. 17, 1962
on 50th Anniversary.

The first concern was to get the kids on the wagon out of the way. Al tried to get to the motorbike and get it started, but he didn't have a fast enough take off. One bull knocked the other right over the top of the bike trashing it. Al was underneath the heap and when he finally got his wits about him his first thought was he was so lucky that one of those bulls horns didn't go right through him.

Some family traditions still hold on the Bruce ranch. The whole family and several neighbors get together for hog butchering day. Everyone helps, but now that they have the old Crum Meat Co. plant it is easier to butcher there, but there is a cold room and meat saws on the Bruce ranch where they cut the meat up. Up to 50 hogs have been butchered in one day, but now they don't do quite that many. Everyone has their job to do. Rendering lard, scraping the guts to make the sausage casings, cutting and wrapping, it is all a family affair.

Cider making day is also a big production on the Bruce ranch when the apples are picked and put through the cider press to make gallons of the golden juice.

The Bruce ranch raise alfalfa and grain and fatten their own cattle out and sell them directly to Alpine or Orvis Brothers packing houses. They also raise many hogs and fatten them for market. It was pretty simple

Al and Nelda Bruce's
wedding picture,
February 14, 1940.

when the Crum Meat Company was right next door to get the hogs and beef to market. They sold first to Royce Meat Co. in Fall River Mills before that. Then they took the hogs to Gazelle. Now they take about 80 hogs a year to Orland, Calif. to be slaughtered.

Life goes on in the busy lives of the Bruce family and everyone does their job to make things work. The life of a rancher is not easy and the work is hard, but Al and Nelda love their way of life and their family, and wouldn't change it for anything.

Always a laugh and a smile on their faces they love to visit and make you feel most welcome to their home.Even the eight little white pigs that crawled through the fence and were trespassing in to the yard were not unwelcome. Al said with a laugh, those little stinkers they aren't suppose to be there.

Glorianne Weigand
March 15, 1996

Over a Century of Ranching

The year was 1858 and young Edward Bosworth worked hard splitting rails for fifty cents a day. His lunch cost him twenty cents a day, but it took a day and a half wages for a pair of pants. Fifty cents for the cloth and twenty-five cents for the tailor to make them. Over a week's worth of wages was needed to buy a pair of $3.75 boots. Forty cents for a sack of wheat and fifty cents for ten pounds of fence nails.

When Edward was twenty-three years old he purchased a marriage license for $1.15 and on January 20, 1860 he took seventeen year old Luthera Coock Farnham as his bride. Edward was politically minded and that same year he did his duty by voting for Abraham Lincoln as President of the United States.

Edward's ancestors had an early start in the United States. Edward is a family name carried down from generation to generation and it is hard to realize how many generations ago it truly was, when in 1634, Great Great Grandparents Edward and Mary Bosworth came to America and settled in Hull, Massachusetts. They with their five children, Jonathan, Nathaniel, Benjamin, Mary and Edward had sailed from England on the ship, Elizabeth and Dorcas. Father, Edward stood six foot six inches tall and was nicknamed "LONG SHANKS". He became quite ill on the long voyage and was dying as the ship neared their port of destination. He was carried to the deck that he might see "Canaan The Promised Land". He died shortly after and was buried in Hull, Massachusetts.

After young Edward and Luthera were married in 1860, Luthera's sister Lucy married Edward's half brother Nathaniel. In 1863 Edward moved his family to Sacramento, California from Illinois. They moved on to Napa County in 1865. They believed Napa was the prettiest place in California. The valley was rich and narrow and surrounded with low hills of the coastal range. There was good feed for their livestock, field crops, vineyards and orchards. Edward planted a large orchard of fruit trees, grapes and a large garden so he might sell produce.

Becoming acquainted with Mr. Stewart who had a homestead in Northern California in a valley named Cayton, the idea of a trade was discussed. Soon a trade was made for the Stewart place in Cayton to the Bosworths in Napa.

In 1880 when Edward and Luthera's son Walter was seven years old they left their pretty place in Napa and moved to another pretty place far to the North.

A beautiful mountain valley about a mile wide and two miles long, rimmed by hills on three sides, open to the sun on the south where a little stream, the overflow of a marsh, tumbles over the rocks into the deep Pit River Canyon. This marsh was formed by water from a spring in the upper end. Indians were native to this land and fished the Pit River for fresh water clams, trout and salmon. The valley was named Cayton after a nephew of General Ulysses Grant, named L. Cayton, who came there to live among the Indians, and marry an Indian woman. They had one son, Malcolm Cayton. L. Cayton built a cabin on the hillside near Cayton Creek. It was there that he was killed by the Indians that he thought were his friends. His son grew to manhood and was a friend to the white settlers.

Pioneers homesteaded the large valley and cleared the brush and trees

The Bosworth home, built in 1900.

to reclaim the marsh land and drained it to make the fertile valley.

The first white people to establish homesteads here were the Snells who came about 1870. Grandma Snells' husband had been killed by runaway horses. The brave, hard working woman raised her seven children on her homestead by the spring in the upper end of the valley on the East side.

On the northwestern side is where Stewart traded his homestead to the Bosworths of Napa County. A barn and a house were on the 160 acres.

Edward and Luthera moved to their new home and planted an orchard. Their family of Carrie, Eugene and Walter were happy in their new homeland. In 1881 Edward's half brother Nathaniel and his wife Lucy moved out from Missouri with their family of Curtis, Mary, Ella, Albert and Gilbert. They settled on the western side of the valley.

On the southeastern side where the road went to Glenburn, Jack Opdyke had a stopping place for travelers. Jack also had the first post office in Cayton. The mail was carried by stage coach or horseback three days a week from Burney.

Others who homesteaded in the valley were Gilbert Tyrrell, Frank House, Blake and Fred Greer, Kentner, Morgan and Aub Burton, Ernie Elder, Charlie Willis, John McIntoch, George Bellinger, Ike Hennegar, Will Malone, Matteo Pasero, Will Farmer, John Bidwell, Harry Wilcox, Levi Lindsey, Clarence and Harry Houston.

Almost all of the residents of the valley were farmers and raised their necessary food. Sugar, salt, coal oil and dry goods were traded for with the excess butter, eggs, poultry, potatoes and meat.

As young Walter Bosworth grew up he favored ranching and as other homesteaders wanted to move on he bought out their claims.

John Bidwell had purchased Curt Bosworth's place and lived there until 1937 when Percy and Elsie Norris moved up from Santa Rosa and bought him out. This is still the Dick and Elouise Norris ranch today.

Cayton was a stopping place for travelers and cowmen driving their beef to the nearest rail head at Bartle. During a severe winter and deep snow a herd of cattle over a half mile long was driven the thirty-five miles from Cayton to Bartle. The drive took two days to move one hundred and fifty head. For fifteen miles the cattle were driven single file through the heavy snow. Horses had been used to break the trail for the slow moving cattle. The heavy drifts were as high as the cows' backs.

The first school in the valley was held in a log cabin which burned. A second school was built and it also burned. A third school was built on Harry Wilcox's ranch and was named "Old Missouri College". Teachers at that time were Carrie Bosworth and Etta Crews.

School was held in the summer and let out in the severe winter in the early years. Later the Fremont school was built halfway down the hill toward the Pit River and the crossing at Peck's Bridge. Teachers were Sadie Hays, Ella P. Braden, Augusta Marsh, Mrs. Hudspeth, Laura Greer and many others. Some teachers boarded with families that lived close by their schools. Later on, school was let out during the crop seasons so the older boys could help in the hay fields and with the harvesting. At the Fremont school a huge bell was rung promptly at 8:30 A.M. by an older student that worked as janitor and came to build the fire to warm the building. The clanging bell could be heard all over the valley and was a cheerful sound.

Cayton Valley was cut off from the Burney side by the raging Pit River. The first crossing was a private ferry. A cable operated a barge in an eddy and the current carried the barge across from side to side whenever anyone came along and wanted to cross. Wagons were floated on the barge and the horses swam the river. The first bridge was built on rock piers.

One time a band of wild horses were being driven south from Oregon into the Sacramento Valley. The man in the lead could not hold them to cross the early bridge slowly and the horses started trotting and the bridge began to bounce. The man barely got across as the middle span collapsed with the horses and bridge falling into the river. Some of the horses fell on the rocks and river and were killed. The surviving horses swam to the north bank to join those remaining horses that had not yet approached the bridge. The frightened horses were rounded up by Bob Farmer and made to swim the river. The school teacher Mrs. Braden, let the school children out to run to the river to see the excitement. The children had watched the band of wild horses as they had passed the school a half mile from the bridge, and could not be kept still with all the commotion going on.

Most ranchers acquired their property by taking up homesteads or timber claims. After a man or woman reached the age of twenty-one anyone could take up a homestead. The requirement was to build a livable house and stay on the property for five years. The homesteader could prove up on the property and was then given a deed. In later years the residence requirement was changed to three years. Homes were built, brush cleared, crops planted and a farm was established. Life was hard, but satisfying. Families were close knit and everyone helped one another.

Wildlife abounded in the valley of Cayton. Deer were plentiful and many bear roamed the forests.

Nathaniel's son Albert (Bert) was twelve when the family moved to Cayton Valley. Bert was not a healthy young man and suffered from hay fever and other problems. On the advice of the local doctor he left the ranch and moved to Fall River Mills around the turn of the century and started a store. The business he founded in 1898 was the oldest one in Eastern Shasta County. The store that Bert started was a success and among other things he sold he also made and sold homemade ice cream. He would cut the ice in the winter from the river and store it in an ice house he had built, stacking it like bricks and covering it in sawdust.

Bert's wife Etta Burner lived only a year after their marriage. Several years later he married Josephine (Jo) Brown and they continued the store business. In 1904 Bert built a new store building on Main Street in Fall River Mills. Sporting goods, jewelry, light plants, pumps and plumbing equipment and electrical supplies were his main sales items. Josephine had been involved in the photography business and that became a large part of their business.

When PG&E started the Pit One project Jo Bosworth became their official photographer and she did a complete pictorial story of the historical event.

Bert had given his ice cream business to his niece Esther Bosworth who had come to help him in the store when his first wife died.

Bert and Jo had a phenomenal collection of photographs that they had

The Bosworth family: top, l. to r., Clarence, Elsie, Wallace, Irene, and Laurence. Front, l. to r., Walter Jr., Walter Sr., Ronald, Lucy, and Edward.

Walter Sr. and Bert Bosworth with a bear Walter Sr. killed in Cayton Valley.

taken and collected through their busy lives.

Twenty years after Edward and Luthera had moved to the homestead traded from Mr. Stewart they built a large home. In 1900, a beautiful three story home which comprised of two complete homes was built, it took two years to complete the house. Edward and Luthera lived in the upstairs section of the house while their son Walter and Lucy and family lived in the downstairs portion of the home. There were eleven large rooms with two full attics.

Walter Scott Bosworth married Lucy Farnham, and by this time he had acquired quite a bit of property in Cayton Valley. Their children Clarence, Irene, Wallace, Laurence, Edwin, Edward, Walter Jr. and Ronald were all born in the valley in the large home.

Clarence only left his beloved Cayton Valley in 1918 when he left to go to the army in World War I. A young school teacher Elsie Lonquist had come to the valley from Goose Creek and boarded at the Walter Bosworth home. When Clarence returned home from the service he married the local school marm. Clarence and Elsie shared a love for music and with Clarence on his violin and Elsie on the organ they started having dances every Saturday night. Lonnie Cleland played with Elsie and Clarence among other musicians and the group was known as "The Bosworth Trio". For forty years they played Saturday night dances from Adin to Montgomery Creek. Elsie and Clarence never had any children.

When Clarence was only seven years old his father raised potatoes and was hauling them to McCloud with teams of mules. Clarence loved to go along and help out. While his father built the campfire and got their meals, it was Clarence's job to tend the mules. Walter decided to put on a second wagon and haul more potatoes at one time. Walter devised a stake on the brake of the wagon so Clarence could lean against it and put on the brake when necessary. The mules knew what to do so holding the reins is all that Clarence had to do.

Walter's family married and some moved on. Irene married Olaf Olson. He had come to the area when PG&E was building a railroad from Bartle to haul material into Hat Two for the Pit One power house construction. The winter of 1921 teamsters hauled their freight and stopped at the ranches along the way at night. The first stop was Bear Flat, then Cayton and Burney Falls. The Red River Lumber company was furnishing power from Susanville for the building of Hat Creek 1 and Hat Creek 2 power houses. There were many men and teams hired. Some of them boarded at Walter Bosworths. Olaf was one of the contractors that boarded there. Irene and Olaf's family consisted of Frederick, Elizabeth, Walter and Donald.

Wallace married Bessie Haynes who was raised at Goose Creek near Burney. Their children were Robert and Wallace Jr. They moved to Red Bluff and were in the sheep business.

Edwin died in infancy.

Edward married Gulda Sill in a double wedding ceremony with Laurence and Ethel. On a trip to Redding during a severe storm with strong winds a big pine tree fell across their car and Edward was killed.

Walter married Florence Quinne and their children were Barbara, James, Lucille and Elsie. Walter loved the outdoor life and went into the hunting, packing and guide service. He later moved his family to Canada where he became a big game guide.

Ronald married Marie Sage and their children were Arleen and Clyde. He enjoyed music and often played saxophone with the Bosworth Trio. He worked on ranches in the area.

Laurence married Ethel Derrick and their children were Melburn (hers from a former marriage) Edward, Lorena, Virginia and Ann.

In 1926 Laurence worked for the Trinity Land and Cattle Co. taking care of their cattle. There he met Ethel and after their marriage they lived in Pondosa. He worked with teams in the woods logging. In 1929 Laurence bought sheep in partnership with Wallace and went to Chico with them for the winter. In 1931 they dissolved their partnership and Laurence returned to the ranch at Cayton Valley. In 1930 a forest fire along the PG&E line, a quarter mile from the ranch threatened their property and driven by west winds the barn and the silo were burned. The wind shifted or the house would have burned also.

In 1943 Laurence moved his family to Anderson where he became active in the trucking business, hauling mostly cattle and hay. Laurence's son Edward could not wait to get out of high school in Anderson and start driving truck for his dad.

He thought that would be the greatest job ever. After a few long hauls Edward crawled out of his truck and quit the job with his dad. Trucking was not for him.

After the death of Walter in 1947 in Cayton Valley, Ronald and Laurence bought out the other heirs and went into partners in 1950. After seven years they decided to dissolve their partnership and Laurence bought out his brother. Laurence's son Edward married Charlene Cole in 1951, his high school sweetheart from Anderson. Charlene spent her early life in Colorado then her family moved to Anderson, California when she was seven years old. Edward and his bride moved to the Bosworth ranch in Cayton Valley and remodeled the cookhouse for their home that Harry Horr had used for years while he had his lumber camp nearby. The logging camp store and office building was built into a bunk house for the Bosworth ranch.

At one time Laurence drove a truck to haul lumber for Horr's mill to Bartle to load onto the train.

Harry Horr had quite a timber operation in the area cutting all the logs and lumber for the Pit 1 power house projects.

Walter Sr. wanted to cut some timber on his property and needed the power to do the job. The McArthur family had a huge steam engine that they had bought to do the farming and build canals to drain the McArthur swamp. The massive machine was too large and cumbersome for the swamp and kept sinking to the bottom. Also the fire burning machine would catch the peat moss on fire. Bosworth bought the gigantic machine from the McArthurs and Levi Lindsay and Laurence Bosworth drove the impractical piece of equipment to Cayton Valley. Two and a half miles an hour was top speed, so the journey took several days. When the machine was first bought by McArthurs it was delivered on the railroad to Bartle and at that time Levi Lindsay was the engineer to drive it to the McArthur swamp.

The intention was to use the steam engine to power a sawmill, but Harry Horr had his sawmill right next to the ranch, so he offered to cut the lumber for Bosworths. It stood for years outside the big gate at the home place being neglected and un-used. The Bosworth family decided to move the McLaughlin Steam engine to the fair-grounds as an exhibit. Still owned by the Bos-worth family, it was loaded onto a low bed truck and was taken to McArthur in the early

Wedding picture of
Charlene and Edward Bosworth, 1951.

208

1950's for all to enjoy. The big red and black steam engine is now considered the logo for the Inter Mountain Fair.

In 1926 Pit River was dammed up and Lake Britton was formed. Before that time there were many farms, ranches and homesteads along the Pit River near Cayton Valley. Many of those homesites are now under the water of Lake Britton.

Young Edward Bosworth, the son of Laurence and Ethel can remember his first school in Cayton Valley. Before Edward was born in 1931 there had been a school down along the Pit River where there was quite a settlement. Edward and his father Laurence had both been born in the big house on the Bosworth ranch. The house is now occupied by Edward Jr. who is the fifth generation Bosworth to work the land and care for the cattle in Cayton Valley in one hundred and sixteen years.

The Bosworth ranch consists of 3100 acres of which 1600 is irrigated meadows, alfalfa and grain lands. The rest is grazing and timber lands. Part of the ranch is on Bear Creek, Clark Creek and Rock Creek. The main water source is Clark Creek, but a huge spring irrigates most of the meadow. Six wheel lines and flood irrigation provide the water for the fields.

When Edward was a young boy he could remember six feet of snow on the valley floor. Now if a foot of snow stacks up it is unusual. At that time all the haying and farming was done with horses. He can remember when his father and grandfather along with the hired men would harness thirty-two head of horses. When Edward was five years old he drove the derrick team to stack the hay. Raising nets to the top of the

Laurence and Ethel Bosworth.

stack to be dumped. A Jackson fork was used to lift the huge loads of hay to be stacked into the barn. Edward said the horses knew more than he did, he just had to tell them when to do it. Four horses were used on each wagon and buck rakes and slides. There were five or six mowing machines at a time in the fields. It was always September before they got done with the haying then it was harvest time. It took six or eight horses to pull the plows to till the soil.

The hired men lived in the bunk house and Ethel did the cooking for them.

Edward rode his horse to school the first year at Clark Creek, then he later rode with the mail carrier. Ethel moved to Burney so it would be easier for the children to go to school. After one year they moved to Cottonwood then to Anderson, coming back to the family ranch and Cayton Valley in 1950.

The Bosworth ranch now runs about six hundred mother cows. With spring and fall calving, the cattle are bred in the meadows and fields at home before ever being turned out on the range. No bulls are ever turned to the allotments. The cattle are shipped to Corning and Red Bluff for the winter and the yearling heifers are kept at home and fed hay. The steers are sent to grass. Quite a bit of the hay produced in Cayton Valley is sold. The cows are brought up from the valley around the first of May. They are taken back to the four different leased pastures in December or January, depending on the year. After coming home in the spring, they graze the meadows during the breeding season then turn the cattle to the high mountains of which twenty per cent is Forest Service and the rest belongs to timber companies. About half the cattle calve in the mountains and the rest calve in the valley, so most of the cattle are hardly ever seen during the calving season, but still a 92% calf crop is experienced.

The cattle from Cayton Valley with the backward LB brand on the right hip are sold on the video satellite through Shasta Livestock Auction. It isn't like years ago when a cow buyer was knocking on your door every few days and stopping in for coffee or at lunch time to see if you had a few old cows to sell, or a load of steers.

Black hided cattle seem to be the trend these days, so Edward buys a lot of good bulls at the Red Bluff Bull Sale. The ranch runs a three way cross with Hereford, Angus and Shorthorn.

Known for having good working cow dogs, Edward was asked to judge the Cow Dog contest at the Red Bluff Bull Sale and for two years he had that job to add to his many others. He said it was hard to please everybody and the only happy one was the winner. One of his jobs is a director of Federal Land Bank for many years. Edward Sr. and Jr. are

Edward Bosworth Sr., 1990.

both active members of the InterMountain Cattlemen, and Charlene is a Past President of the InterMountain CattleWomen.

In 1965 potatoes were grown in Cayton Valley by Orin Kaylor and Jess Brown. They had been grown on a smaller scale years ago when Clarence drove the mules to Bartle. In the fall the potatoes were dug and trucked to the sorting sheds in McArthur where others were raising potatoes. They were boxed and sacked and stamped Cayton Valley potatoes. In 1966 Laurence, Edward Sr. Orin Kaylor and Edward Jr. raised potatoes again. The price was very low, so they stored the potatoes in a barn until spring only to find the price even less. Today only cattle and hay are raised on the Bosworth ranch, and it seems the cattle prices are going the same direction of the potato prices in 1966.

Laurence died in 1980, but Ethel still lives on her ranch in Anderson, Calif. Edward laughs and says she is so busy with Bingo that he has to make an appointment to see her.

Edward Sr. and Charlene have two sons, Larry who is an investment manager for a bank in Medford, Oregon and Edward Jr. who works on the ranch. Today the fourth, fifth and sixth generation of Edward Sr., Edward Jr. and his son Dan live and work on the ranch. A heritage that they can be proud of.

Glorianne Weigand
April 24, 1996